AVISSON YOUNG ADULT SERIES

The Experimenters

Twelve Great Chemists

Margery Evernden

Avisson Press, Inc
Greensboro

First edition
Printed in the United States of America
ISBN 1-888105-49-6

Library of Congress Cataloging-in-Publication Data

Evernden, Margery.
    The experimenters : twelve great chemists / Margery Evernden.
        p. cm. -- (Avisson young adult series)
    Includes bibliographical references and index.
    ISBN 1-888105-49-6 (pbk.)
        1. Chemists--Biography--Juvenile literature. 2. Chemistry--
    History--Juvenile literature.
    [1. Chemists. 2. Chemistry--History.] I. Title. II. Series.

    QD21 .E94 2001
    540'.92'2--dc21
    [B]

                                            00-052601

*In proud memory of
Earl A. Gulbransen,
chemist*

Table of Contents

Once Upon a Time....

Chemistry is the science which studies substances and the changes they undergo. It has been called the "divine science." It has also been called the "swindler science."

Over the years chemists have been rich, poor, honored, exiled, even beheaded. They have shamelessly laid claim to the ideas of others and have nobly given up their lives.

Chemistry's ancestors include Tapputi, mistress of household and perfumeress of ancient Mesopotamia; the secretive artisans of old Egypt, makers of dyes and perfumes, workers in metals; Arricenna, the Arab "prince of all learning"; the alchemists in both East and West who for centuries sought the elixir of eternal youth and the way to turn base metals into gold — these and, also, the towering philosopher/naturalist Aristotle, born in 384 B.C.E..

Aristotle took all knowledge as his domain but would have refused to touch a test tube or retort. He believed with earlier Greeks that the physical universe is made up of four "elements" - earth, air, fire and water. These "elements" have four "attributes" — heat and cold, wetness and dryness. Earth is cold and dry. Water is wet and cold. Air or wind is warm and moist. Fire is hot and dry. In their many combinations, Aristotle declared, "elements" account for the multitude of objects which we see around us in the natural world.

These beliefs dominated Western thought for two thousand years. They were based upon logic and reason. Experiments, if conducted at all, were important only as they said "Yes" to ideas already held.

But human curiosity could not forever be confined in a strait jacket.

By the sixteenth century C.E., daring investigators were challenging both the alchemists and the Greeks.

In England in the seventeenth century, the lavishly educated Robert Boyle, seventh son of the great Earl of Cork, devoted his life to the study of science and religion. Like the alchemists before him, Boyle believed that lead could be turned into silver and gold, but he preached and practiced experimentation. To support experimental scientists, he helped to found the Invisible College which later became the Royal Society of London, active to this day.

In Germany the bitter and melancholy George Ernest Stahl wrote many of his strange papers in a mixture of German, Latin and alchemistic symbols. Abandoning the notion of "fire as an element," he proposed a startling new theory of combustion or burning.

In Russia, at the beginning of the eighteenth century, a fisherman's child, Mikhail Vasilevich Lomonosov, arrived penniless in Moscow and lied his way to the excellent education which by law was available only to noblemen's sons. Lomonosov was at times a prisoner doing his scientific work behind bars. At other times he was the master of a splendid estate with a hundred serfs. He wrote poetry, reorganized Russian grammar, worked in chemistry, physics and mathematics and founded the University of Moscow. "Lomonosov was himself a university," it was said. He was a leading champion of experimentation.

By the mid-eighteenth century it was clear that scientific advance depended not simply on brilliant thinkers but also on practical work in the laboratory. Experiments must be carried on through meticulous measurement and unbiased observation, accurately recorded. Scientists performing the same experiment anywhere in the world should arrive at the same result. Furthermore, truly important scientific work would not only solve a particular problem. It would raise a host of new questions.

The stage was set for the appearance of "the father of modern chemistry," the French genius Antoine Laurent Lavoisier.

Chapter I
Antoine Lavoisier
Father of Modern Chemistry

It was the year 1743.

In the glittering palace of Versailles, King Louis XV of France was in the thirty-fifth year of his long and extravagant reign. His chief demand of his engineers was that they provide ever and ever more water for the royal fountains.

In the city of Paris thousands of Louis' subjects were living in dark rooms on narrow, twisting alleyways, unlighted at night, running with filth and ordure night and day. A constant danger was their water, carted by unwashed men and animals and sold in the noisome streets.

In the lovely mansions clustered near the Old Louvre palace near the banks of the River Seine, rich Parisians guarded their comforts but were saddened by the excesses of their King. Some of them hoped and planned for a better France.

In one such mansion on the quiet Cul-de-Sac Pecquet a baby boy was born on an August day. At three o'clock that afternoon he was carried to the ancient parish church of Saint Merry's for christening. The baby's father was Jean-Antoine Lavoisier, descendant of peasants but himself risen to high position as law officer of the Crown. The mother was Émilie Punctis, the daughter of a lawyer and secretary to a Vice-Admiral of France.

The new-born boy was christened Antoine Laurent.

Two years later a daughter was born to the Lavoisiers. In 1748 the frail young mother died. Father Jean with his two small children went to live on the Rue de Four-St. Eustache with his recently widowed mother-in-law. In that fine house the children were adoringly tended by their Aunt Constance, their mother's younger sister.

When he was eleven years old Antoine was enrolled as a day pupil at the College Mazarin. There he studied Latin, Greek and French literature, tried unsuccessfully to write a play and won second prize for a serious essay entitled "Is uprightness as essential as accuracy in research?"

Already it was scientific research which fascinated the boy.

His teacher in mathematics and astronomy was the Abbé de Lacaille who had spent four years at the Cape of Good Hope on the southernmost tip of Africa, trying to measure the length of an earthly meridian. In Lacaille's life and teachings Antoine glimpsed a world of order and simplicity which thrilled and challenged him.

But science was a hobby, not a career, so Father Jean declared. Antoine was no rebel against a father who was his dearest friend, nor did he wish to be poor. At eighteen he obediently entered the Paris Law School, though he resolved to pursue science as well.

To make sure that no one interrupted his many studies, Antoine soon announced that he was ill and could not receive visitors. One rejected friend sent him a bowl of gruel and a note which declared that "One year on earth is worth a hundred in the memory of man."

Antoine did not change his ways. He was neither a natural hermit nor a curmudgeon. He was in fact a pleasant young man, slender, with fine features and red hair or brown; accounts differ. Always at ease in society, he was also fiercely dedicated.

He studied botany with Bernard de Juissieu who had begun to classify plants according to the new and sensible system proposed by the Swedish scientist Linnaeus.

He studied chemistry with Guillaume François Rouelle whose colorful lectures attracted even fashionable aristocrats who came to see the famous Rouelle "strip tease." Rouelle always began his stuttering lecture-demonstrations dressed like a proper eighteenth century gentleman, but in his excitement he gradually threw off his hat, his powdered wig, his cravat, his jacket. Often he went into his storage room for further supplies and returned to his audience with never a break in his lecture. Rouelle inspired his precocious student.

It was, however, the gruff mineralogist and geologist, Jean-Etienne Guettard who rescued Antoine from a legal career. Guettard was a "Hottentot in society," as he himself boasted, but he came to the select gatherings of friends at old Madame Punctis' home. There he developed a deep interest in Madame Punctis' grandson. He took the boy on brief geologic expeditions. On Antoine's completion of law school he offered him a job helping to map the Île de France, locating quarries, mineral and rock supplies and studying stream water.

Antoine spent his small salary not on wigs and silken britches but on barometers, thermometers and hydrometers which he set up in the family mansion. Using these instruments, he kept daily records of temperatures, air pressure and moisture content. He trained his father and loyal Aunt Constance to take readings when he himself was away from home. Throughout his life Antoine would record readings of his own and from correspondents as far away as Aleppo and Baghdad. With such knowledge it should be possible to predict weather, he believed.

In 1765 when he was just twenty-two years old Antoine presented his first scientific paper before the Academy of Science. The paper was entitled the "Analysis of Gypsum."

Gypsum was a mineral which, when heated, could be

ground to a fine white powder. That powder grew soft when combined with water, then hardened to the "plaster of Paris" widely used in the construction of Parisian buildings. How did gypsum so mysteriously "set," Antoine wondered. His answer was not strikingly different from previous research, but his paper showed a talent for careful measurement and a determination to report only what experiment proved.

In that same year 1765, the government offered a prize for an essay on street lighting. Antoine knew that when he and his friends went out into nighttime Paris, they had to be accompanied by servants carrying torches before them. Into some black alleys they dared not go at all.

He set about studying the lamps then available. He measured their efficiencies, estimated their costs and suggested — with a solid Lavoisier respect for money — how they could be financed. He offered no original solution, but for his meticulous collection of information he was awarded a gold medal "by order of the King."

Now real adventure loomed. In 1767 Antoine undertook with his friend Guettard a thousand mile geologic expedition to Alsace and Lorraine. The roads of the region were too poor for carriages. They were, in addition, infested with bandits, or so Father Jean and Aunt Constance feared. Guettard, Antoine and a Lavoisier family servant set out on horseback, pistols prominently protruding from their coat pockets.

No bandits appeared, but Guettard wrote to Father Jean that "One has to be made of iron for this trade." The three travelers were alternately drenched with rain and soaked with sweat. The sun, when it shone, was so hot that they were "grilled like herring....Such are the joys of mineralogy."

Antoine wrote to his family regularly and cheerfully. He reported that he rode up mountains "barometer in hand" and directed that his father bring a bowl of gold fish as a gift for a friend when he came to meet the travelers near the end of their journey. Father Jean dutifully brought the gold fish.

Unfortunately, although Guettard was a devoted geologist, he was a poor politician. He was never paid for this work. The records of the expedition were not published for some years and then without mentioning either Guettard or Lavoisier.

But Antoine had by now inherited enough money to buy books and good scientific equipment. At twenty-five he was elected to the Academy of Science. A commoner — although his father would later buy him a minor title of nobility — he was at first obliged to sit silently in a back seat at the Academy meetings. Undaunted, he was soon busy with Academy work.

Antoine sought a method for improving the Parisian water brought from the River Seine, then muddy and impure. He grandly proposed diverting the unpolluted waters of the River Yvette.

Through the years he would make reports for the Academy on a breath-taking array of subjects. Among them were bleaching, paper, fossils, an invalid chair, a tobacco grater, the site of the public slaughter-houses, the working of coal mines, the cultivation of cabbage, glass, Chinese ink, volcanoes, meteorites, white soap, animal magnetism, and the newly-invented air balloon.

One especially momentous step Antoine took only a few days after he became a member of the Academy. He joined the *Ferme Generale*, the organization which collected the taxes of France.

Tax collectors are never loved in any country. They were detested by the over-burdened people of France.

Antoine had often visited his father's native village of Villers-Cotterets. There he had seen bare-footed peasants painfully bending to sow their meager crops. Nearby the large and beautiful forest of Villers-Cotterets, rich with game, was reserved for the hunting parties of the Duc d'Orleans. On his trip with Guettard Antoine had seen peasants wrenched from their ripening harvests to work unpaid upon the royal highways. He was not and never would be indifferent to the sufferings of the common people.

Yet science was his passion and the service he could render to his country. Even an honest tax collector, and Antoine seems to have been one of those, could gain great wealth, a sure way to finance scientific research.

Antoine gained yet another treasure as a result of his membership in the Ferme. At the home of Jacques Paulze, a respected older "farmer," he met his new friend's fourteen-year-old daughter Marie Anne Pierette.

Marie was pretty, intelligent and eager to escape marriage to a middle-aged count whom she called an "aggressive ogre." She was equally eager to become a helpmate to the young genius Lavoisier. The two were married in 1771.

The teen-aged bride set about learning English and Latin so that she could translate scientific papers for her husband who, with all his gifts, was not clever at languages. She worked at his side in the laboratory. She took drawing lessons from the great painter David so that she could illustrate Antoine's voluminous laboratory notes. David painted the couple in a portrait now owned by the Metropolitan Museum in New York. The portrait shows Marie, slender and lovely, standing beside her husband, her arm upon his shoulder. Antoine, seated at his desk, looks up at her as if asking for advice or approval.

Antoine has sometimes been called rigidly logical, cold and "inaccessible." Clearly Marie did not find him so. All her life she herself was fiery in both love and hate.

When Antoine became a member of the Gunpowder

Commission, charged with developing French sources of saltpetre for the making of armaments, the young couple moved into an apartment in the Arsenal. There Antoine set up at his own expense the greatest laboratory of the eighteenth century world equipped with some 15,000 precision instruments and pieces of chemical apparatus. There he cooperated with other researchers, financing many of them. He also helped support his crusty old friend Guettard.

Visitors came to the Arsenal laboratory from Europe and America. Some were eager to take part in lively scientific discussion, some to carry on their own work, some to watch their host perform his ingenious experiments. One visitor, Benjamin Franklin of Philadelphia, had his portrait painted by Marie. He sent her a witty thank you note, delayed, so he apologized, by a touch of gout!

Antoine, with study and routine work behind him, was now in the great creative period of his life. For twenty years he designed and performed a series of experiments which laid the groundwork for chemical research to modern times.

As early as 1767, Antoine had disproved a two-thousand-year-old dictum of Aristotle. Since elements could be turned one into another, the Greeks had said, water could be turned to earth by heating.

Turning to a piece of apparatus used by the alchemists, Antoine poured rain water into a two-handled glass "pelican." Once he had siphoned away the air he securely stoppered the pelican. He then weighed the vessel, set it in a sand bath and gently heated it from below by an olive oil lamp kept at constant temperature.

After 101 patient days Antoine removed the lamp, let the pelican cool and again weighed it on a delicate balance. The stoppered pelican had not lost its weight. *But an unstoppered pelican also heated had lost weight.* Furthermore, the tiny flecks of matter which had collected at the bottom of the heated vessel were not earth. They were particles from the glass. *Water had not turned and would not turn into earth.* Furthermore, it could be accurately analyzed.

"The more extraordinary facts are, the more they distance themselves from received and accepted opinions, the more important it is to state them by repeated experiments in such a way as to leave no doubt," said Antoine.

Repeated experiment would be his watchword. Precise weight measurement would be his tool.

Antoine was now approaching new understandings. He discarded forever Aristotle's four "elements." An "element," he decided, is any substance which cannot be decomposed into other simpler substances. A compound is made up of two or more elements which together form a new substance. Furthermore, a fundamental principle of chemistry is the Law of the Conservation of Mass or the Law of the Indestructibility of Matter.

Matter cannot be destroyed. In any chemical operation in a closed system an equal quantity of matter exists both before and after the operation.

Antoine now openly announced his intention of creating a revolution in chemistry.

It was true that the new chemistry must build on work done by many researchers. Antoine was at times accused of using the work of others without giving them due credit. He did not apologize. To him what was important was obtaining accurate experimental data and organizing these facts into a logical and useful order.

In 1771, the year of his marriage, he began what would become his most famous work — a study of combustion or burning. Ever since human beings had observed the results of fire - the flaming paths of volcanic lava, forests reduced to stumps and ash, raw food cooked to be more delectable, metals melted from their rocky matrices — the process of burning had been an awesome mystery. In Antoine's youth the accepted explanation was George Ernest Stahl's hundred year old phlogiston theory.

According to that theory, which had sprung from philosophy, not experimentation, a "spirit of fire" or phlogiston escapes into the air during burning. Human beings give off phlogiston when they breathe. Metals when heated give off this "spirit of fire," which cannot be caught or weighed. A highly combustible material like charcoal must contain a great deal of phlogiston. When charcoal is heated with the ash or calyx of a metal, the original metal will be regenerated.

Antoine's flamboyant and beloved teacher Rouelle had given many demonstrations which seemed to uphold the phlogiston theory. Yet as time went by the pupil was not satisfied. He began his first investigations of combustion with experiments on diamonds.

He discovered that diamonds when heated in a carefully sealed container browned slightly on the surface but remained intact. Diamonds heated *in air* behaved very differently. *They disappeared.*

The latter fact had already been observed. Antoine repeated the experiment, using for his source of heat a giant burning lens. Yes, in open air the diamond vanished. What had happened? Perhaps an invisible gas had been formed? Antoine placed diamonds again under the burning lens, this time enclosing them in air but in a vessel which could capture any gas given off.

In twenty minutes the diamonds had vanished — and the enclosing vessel did indeed contain a weighable gas. That gas was at the time called "fixed air." Today it is known as carbon dioxide.

Antoine had proved that the sparkling diamond is a

simple chemical substance much like black charcoal. The finding angered many scientists who by now saw the phlogiston theory begin to totter.

Antoine was wounded by an attack from the aged Rouelle, but he did not change course.

He proceeded to test phosphorous, the first element to have been deliberately prepared and isolated in the laboratory some hundred years before. Phosphorous means "light-burning." Everyone had seen its glow. When heated, this element, so Antoine's balance told him, *absorbed air. And its weight increased by exactly the weight of that air.* Once again no elusive and unweighable "spirit of fire"!

On then to heating and weighing of sulphur. The same story!

Antoine was now resolved to prove by experiment that all metals when reduced to ashes or calx gain weight from the air. Experiments on tin and lead were lengthy and sometimes dangerous. Antoine was forced to work wearing an iron mask and goggles. But he continued to get the results which he had predicted.

Many more remarkably designed experiments were to come. There were also to be many painful questions, as Antoine's extensive laboratory notes reveal. There would be much careful reasoning and, yes, some unacknowledged borrowings from his great English rival, Joseph Priestley. So Antoine arrived at last at his revolutionary theory of combustion.

Common air, he announced, is a compound. It is made up almost entirely of "mephitic air," today called nitrogen, and "pure air" to which he gave the name oxygen. Placed in nitrogen candles go out, creatures die. Placed in oxygen candles burn merrily and life continues, as captive mice and birds conveniently proved.

A heated substance then burns by absorbing oxygen from

the air; combustion cannot take place without oxygen. A heated substance gains in weight by the weight of the absorbed oxygen.

The theory, so startling to eighteenth century science, is proved afresh by every cook who forces a cover upon a skillet of burning fat. No oxygen, no flame!

Every one who has been lulled to sleep before a log fire in a closed room also demonstrates the correctness of the "new chemistry." For Antoine proved by experiments that respiration — breathing — is a kind of combustion. True this combustion is very slow and takes place in the lungs, all unseen, but it is not fundamentally different from the burning of charcoal. Arterial blood is red because it has absorbed oxygen. Respiration, among other things, accounts for the fact that a healthy human being maintains the same body temperature whether shipping aboard an ice breaker to the Arctic or riding astride a camel in the Sahara desert.

Understanding of combustion brought Antoine his greatest fame. Yet he made other vital contributions to chemistry. He discovered the composition of water, which is not, after all, an element but a compound made up of two parts hydrogen and one part oxygen. He helped to create a new chemical vocabulary or nomenclature. There must be "exact expressions" when naming substances, he said. No more fanciful powder of algaroth, butter of antimony or flowers of zinc! The latter two with their pleasant names were, in fact, deadly poisons.

The alchemists, like many ancient artisans, had used mystifying language in order to keep their secrets. Antoine and his co-workers wanted a language which could be understood by chemists anywhere at any time. They presented to the Academy of Science a chart using some traditional names of substances but adding new meaningful names, all logically arranged.

Antoine now set about writing *Un traité de chimie* or, as the English translation was titled, *Elements of Chemistry,* in a new systematic order containing all the modern discoveries. The landmark book was published in France in 1789. The chemical revolution was under way.

Alas for Antoine, another kind of Revolution was sweeping France.

Extravagant King Louis had died dreadfully of smallpox. His body was swiftly buried in quicklime, unmourned by his subjects. His grandson, the young King Louis XVI, briefly seemed to offer hope of a better government for the bankrupt nation.

Antoine, active in politics and economics as in chemistry, believed that reform without revolution was possible. Long-denied rights must be granted to the French poor. Their hard labor must be rewarded, their ancient burdens lightened. Nobles must share those burdens.

But neither young King Louis nor his nobles proved wise or generous enough to change the government and to meet the increasing demands of the indignant people. Far-sighted ministers were appointed but soon left office, their good intentions defeated. The King grew ever and ever more unpopular. Anti-royalist writings flooded the country.

Radical leaders arose. Eight hundred public gibbets for hanging "enemies of the people" were erected in Paris. Then came the guillotine, that terrible, descending knife. With it the new Reign of Terror cut off the heads of King Louis, his wife and children.

The monarchy was ended. Now new and even more violent reformers began to attack any person who had been prominent in the Old Regime. The tax collectors of the

Ferme Generale, of which Antoine had long been a member, were a natural target.

Bloodthirsty Jean Paul Marat, who was himself soon to die by an assassin's blade, directed a fiery blast against Antoine. "I denounce to you," he wrote in his newspaper, "Lavoisier, son of a landgrabber, apprentice-chemist... Farmer General, Commissioner for Gunpowder and Saltpetre, Governor of the Discount Bank, Secretary to the King, Member of the Academy of Science, Bloodsucker... Would to heaven he had been strung to the lamppost."

The "bloodsucker" Lavoisier and all the "farmers" were thrown into prison, accused of withholding a huge sum of money from the state. Their personal wealth was confiscated.

No matter that Antoine was the greatest scientist in France, with important work unfinished. No matter that he had purchased land to carry on agricultural experimentation in the hope of bettering the methods and the lives of French peasants. No matter that he had worked for better lighting and pure drinking water for the people of Paris. No matter that he had studied the grim prisons of his city and recommended new buildings and humane treatment for the prisoners who were, after all, he had pointed out, human beings and subjects of France.

No matter that he had found Parisian hospitals nearly as filthy and overcrowded as the prisons and drawn up a plan for change. No matter that he had recommended health insurance for elderly citizens. No matter that he had developed native mining of saltpetre so that in time of war France could protect herself against attacks from abroad.

No matter even that the charges against the Ferme Generale were false. The "farmers" did not in fact owe money to the state. The state was in debt to them.

Proud Marie Lavoisier refused to grovel before her

husband's and her father's accusers. Antoine was innocent, she declared. All the "farmers" were innocent. All should be released. Antoine would be ashamed to receive his freedom if his fellows were not set at liberty, too.

But the Reign of Terror was at its height. Prisoners on trial were no longer allowed defense lawyers or the right to call witnesses. Judges conducted cases as they saw fit. Juries were merciless. The penalty for all convicted "criminals" was death. Every day clumsy carts laden with victims rumbled over the cobblestone streets of Paris on their way from prison to guillotine.

In the end the members of the *Ferme Generale* were convicted on the fictional charge that they had given financial aid to the enemies of France.

On May 8, 1784, the tumbrels rolled once more, carrying Antoine and the other "farmers" to the Place de la Revolution. There one by one with quiet dignity the prisoners bent their heads to the guillotine's great knife.

Antoine was obliged to watch the execution of his long time friend and father-in-law. Then he himself stepped forward to die.

"Only a moment to cut off that head and a hundred years may not give us another like it," said a sorrowing colleague the next day.

Like a mad and bloody dream, the Reign of Terror soon ended. Order was restored to France. But Antoine's body lay tumbled in a common grave.

His fame could not be buried.

The work of many men contributed to the chemical revolution of the 18th century. It was Antoine Lavoisier who wove the many strands of knowledge into a single useful fabric. It is he who is known as "the father of modern chemistry."

Chapter II

Joseph Priestley

Diligent Experimenter and Furious Free Thinker

J oseph Priestley, founder of the chemistry of gases and Antoine Lavoisier's great rival, was born on March 13, 1733, near Leeds, a busy English market town of 16,000. His father was a cottage weaver, poor, patient and cheerful.

Priestley hardly remembered his mother. When he was six years old, she died, dreaming of heaven and murmuring, "Let me go to that fine place." Three years later, the little boy was sent to live with his father's sister, Aunt Sarah Keighley of Old Hall, Heckmondwike.

Old Hall was three hundred years old, stone-built with a spreading slate roof. Generations of human beings and sick and birthing animals had been warmed at its great fireplace.

Aunt Sarah herself was a hospitable woman. Neighboring housewives were regularly welcomed to Old Hall for prayer meetings. Dissenting ministers were often invited to dinner. Dissenters, a pious but rebellious lot who refused to join the Church of England, often dissented with each other. Aunt Sarah welcomed them all so long as she considered them good and honest men. Her young nephew listened in on their lively arguments.

He was a serious boy. When he was small, he saw wicked spirits in the darkness. There must have been much darkness in the big old house with its narrow windows and flickering candlelight. He believed that he himself was wicked, too, since, try as he might, he could not manage to feel personally guilty for Adam's disobedience to God in the Garden of Eden.

As he grew a little older, the boy decided that there were no wicked spirits. He also decided that he did not need to feel guilty for Adam's misbehavior. God was infinitely good and forgiving. Also, God was one, not the three-in-one deity in whom Aunt Sarah believed. Common sense showed that one and three could never be the same, he decided.

Already Joseph Priestley had become an honest heretic. But he did not reject Aunt Sarah's ambition for him. Aunt Sarah was determined that he should become a dissenting minister.

He went obediently to school. Rules required that boys attend classes eight hours a day, their hands and faces must be washed, their hair or periwigs combed, their boots blacked. They were to rise from their seats and bow whenever a grownup appeared. They were not "to Sware, Lye or hit each other."

Young Priestley studied algebra, geometry and mathematics, Latin, Greek and Hebrew, also Caldean, Syrian and a little Arabic. Outside of class he taught himself what were then called "the polite languages," French, Italian and German. He was scornful of light reading. *Robinson Crusoe* was the only "romance" he read before he was nineteen.

When his local schooling ended, Priestley had to choose a college. Oxford and Cambridge, England's famous old universities, were closed to dissenters. Besides, they were not to Priestley's liking. He was equally opposed to nearby Mile End Academy which trained ministers. There, every student was obliged twice a year to declare his continuing belief in ten strict and unchanging principles.

In the end, Aunt Sarah agreed to let him attend liberal

Daventry Academy. He arrived happily at the college in September 1752, with the required supply of candles and bed sheets. Years later with his usual frankness he would write to the British Prime Minister, "while your universities resemble pools of stagnant water, secured by dams and mounds, ours [the dissenters'] are like rivers which, taking their natural course, fertilize a whole country."

Daventry taught young men — even Daventry did not enroll young women — by free discussion. Religious and ethical questions were addressed in lively debates. The Academy taught no classical languages, though Priestley and his roommate climbed out of bed each morning, well before the 6:10 rising bell, to read ten pages of Greek.

The Academy offered as good a formal scientific education as could be found in 18th century England, but there was no chemistry course. Priestley later decided that he was lucky not to carry the burden of other people's chemical ideas and prejudices.

He was about to take on other burdens. He left Daventry in 1755 to become a minister in Needham Market where the chapel was small and poor. The young clergyman, though bravely dressed in his black coat, powdered wig and tricorned hat, received a near-starvation wage. Aunt Sarah could no longer afford to help him.

To his further distress, the dissenters at Needham Market were shocked at his free thought, particularly his belief in the Unity of God. And they did not like his stammer!

That stammer had plagued him all his life. He might try to persuade himself that the speech impediment was a blessing in disguise since it kept him from the temptation of becoming an empty orator. Unfortunately, it also kept many of the pews in his chapel empty and it kept nearby congregations from inviting him to preach.

Priestley turned to his books, especially to the Bible, and

began his long series of theological writings. Putting words onto paper came easily to him, and he often wrote until he could hardly hold the pen.

After three hungry years he was invited to become a minister at a chapel in the lively market town of Nantwick in Cheshire.

Life grew brighter, his salary a bit higher. He started a small school and discovered that he liked to teach. He unpacked his globes of the earth, bought an air pump, an electric machine and other simple pieces of apparatus. With these he gave scientific demonstrations to the pupils and their parents.

Most important for his private life he met Mary Wilkinson. She was an intelligent young woman, the older sister of one of his students and the daughter of a prosperous iron maker. In 1761 he was hired as a teacher of languages at the Dissenter Academy in Warrington where Mary joined him. A year after the marriage, a daughter, Aunt Sarah's namesake, was born. Now full of enthusiasm for teaching, Priestley set up a new and larger school enrolling both boys and girls.

Unlike most people in the eighteenth century he believed in education for women. He also believed in women having leisure time in which to read.

Mary Priestley, busy supervising the Priestley household, may sometimes have wondered where *she* could find leisure for reading. She made one attempt to send her husband out shopping with a large market basket. There is no record of exactly how he performed the task but she never sent him again. He himself said that he was a lodger in their home. Luckily, Mary had a wry sense of humor. Besides, she could not accuse her husband of being lazy. He was a busy author and teacher.

He liked young people for their openness to new ideas.

He thought their education should be practical, fitting them for the real worlds of commerce and government. He rejected English grammar based on Latin. He taught his students to look at how eighteenth century writers were using the language, and he wrote a Grammar which was popular throughout England for many years. He taught science, or, as it was then called, natural philosophy, by having students do experiments, perhaps the first teacher to do so.

For his history class he published a Chart of Biography listing the great men who had lived from 1100 B.C.E. to 1800 C.E. It was a highly original idea for the time. On publication of the Chart, Priestley was awarded an honorary doctor's degree by the University of Edinburgh.

He sat in on a series of lectures on chemistry and began yearly visits to London where he met important mathematicians and scientists. One of these was Benjamin Franklin who had come to England seeking greater freedom for the American colonies. Franklin's experiments with kite flying in Philadelphia thunderstorms had been undertaken to prove that lightning and electricity were the same. These famous experiments were, in fact, the least of the American's work in the field of electricity, then a subject of intense scientific interest.

For all his stammer and plain country bearing, Priestley was never shy about presenting his own ideas. He confided to Franklin a secret project. He would like to write a history of electricity.

Franklin was encouraging. Priestley went home to write, in a little over a year, his *History and Present State of Electricity.* In his study of other men's work, he found many unanswered questions. Why not look for answers himself? For the first time he performed and wrote about small experiments of his own.

The *History of Electricity* attracted so much attention that the country parson and school teacher was elected a fellow of England's prestigious Royal Society.

Now he had an even more audacious plan. He wanted to write the histories of all the sciences!

Even for hard-working Priestley the project was vast. Orders for his quickly-written *History of Optics* came in slowly and he had no money to continue the series. He did manage to publish a brief *Theory and Practice of Perspective* in which, among other instructions, he recommended the India rubber erasers sold by a London merchant. Up to that time, draftsmen had used bread crumbs for erasers.

Meanwhile, life was changing. In 1867, Priestley became minister at Mill Hill Chapel in Leeds. Here he was at home among people who knew him and liked him. Although he would never quite conquer his pesky stammering, his preaching was successful.

He soon busied himself continuing the long series of theological books and pamphlets which would bring him fame and infamy as his country's leading Unitarian thinker.

But another career awaited him. In his mid-thirties, Joseph Priestley was about to become the founder of pneumatic chemistry, the chemistry of gases, or "airs" as gases were then called.

Next door to the Priestleys' home on Meadow Lane in Leeds was the brewery of Jakes and Nell. Always curious, Priestley noticed that fermenting vats of beer gave off "fixed air." This was the gas which, thanks to Lavoisier's orderly new method of naming chemicals, was to be called carbon dioxide.

What would happen, Priestley wondered, if trays of water were put in the fermenting vats. Jakes and Nell were willing to cooperate with his proposed experiment which did not, after all, damage the beer. To Priestley's delight, his water absorbed great bubbles of the escaping carbon dioxide.

The surprising brew was safe to drink but foul tasting. Priestley devised a method of making carbon dioxide by mixing chalk and sulfuric acid. He introduced this carbon dioxide into water through a flexible tube.

With a rapid series of experiments, he produced a carbonated water which was pleasant to drink. As usual with him, he promptly published a pamphlet about his discovery. He hoped that his new drink might be a cure for scurvy, the dread disease which weakened and killed sailors long at sea. He took the drink to the British Navy who installed it on two of its vessels.

Alas, the drink was not a cure. In 1795, the Navy would end the scourge of scurvy by serving not Priestley's brew but lemon juice, later lime juice, to its sailors.

Priestley's medical hopes were dashed but he had created soda water. Today, people around the world clamor for carbonated drinks in an array of colors and flavors that even he could not have imagined.

Scientists of the eighteenth century recognized three states of matter : solids, liquids and gases. They could not, of course, know that solids keep their volume and shape because the atoms of which they are composed are so tightly packed. The atoms of water and other liquids are less tightly held together. As a result, liquids retain their volume but change shape according to the shape of their containers, whether river bank or drinking glass. The atoms of gases, on the other hand, are so widely separated and loosely held together that they easily drift apart to fill any available space, large or small — dirigible or party balloon. Many gases are invisible.

Their mystery fascinated Priestley. "I am no theorist," he declared, but experiment delighted him. He was endlessly patient and ingenious.

One of the most intriguing mysteries involving gases was that of human and animal breathing. Priestley's experiments showed that mice died and candle flames went out when they had no supply of fresh air. He found, however, that when placed in a container with living plants, mice lived and candles went on burning. He tried mint, balm and even some plants whose names he did not know. These plants differed somewhat in their effects, spinach being the most active, but all, *when placed in sunlight*, kept "atmosphere sweet and wholesome." Clearly, plants breathed out gases which animals and humans needed to survive. Without plants, the atmosphere of the Earth itself would, over time, become poisoned by animal respiration and by animal dying and decaying.

Priestley had discovered what we today call photosynthesis.

The constant and unglamorous problem of his life remained: money! He now had three much loved children, Sally, Joseph, Jr., and William. There would be another son. Mary was not well. Books and chemical experiments were expensive. How to go on?

For a few brief weeks the problem seemed miraculously solved. Priestley was invited to be the astronomer on perhaps the greatest sea voyage ever made — Captain Cook's second voyage around the world. Assured that his family would be well-provided for during his absence, he was eager to visit the wonders of the Antipodes: New Zealand, Tahiti and those other far parts of the globe.

Unfortunately for Priestley, clergymen of the established church were helping chose personnel for Cook's voyage.

These gentlemen distrusted the free-thinking minister. They forced the withdrawal of his nomination.

It was a warning of the kind which Priestley would never heed. He was not unhappy for long. He believed, after all, that in the end everything in the world worked out for the best.

Help came from William Petty, Earl of Shelburne, who lived on a splendid estate at Calme in Wiltshire. Lord Shelburne was a hard and difficult man but he was brave, intelligent and much interested in science. He invited Priestley to become his librarian offering him a comfortable home and a salary two-and-a-half times his minister's pay. He also promised a pension for life.

In eighteenth century England science was subsidized by rich, private citizens. These men were often themselves amateur "natural philosophers." Joseph Priestley was not embarrassed by Lord Shelburne's offer. In 1793, at the age of forty, he moved gratefully to Calme.

His duties were light. Lord Shelburne treated him as a friend, not a servant and provided a laboratory at the end of his own long library. Mary was, at last, spared the stench and fire hazards of her husband's work.

In his new haven, Priestley plunged into his beloved experiments. He also set about writing his masterpiece, *Experiments and Observations on Different Kinds of Air*.

Within a few years, he would prepare an array of crucial chemicals which no one had recognized before. He would find "nitrous air" or nitric oxide; "diminished nitrous air" or nitrous oxide, the laughing gas that would prove a useful anesthetic; "acid air" or hydrochloric acid; "alkaline air" or ammonia; "phlogisticated air" or nitrogen; "vitriolic acid air" or sulphur dioxide. The names he used make hard reading today but the discoveries remain.

As always, his work was not principally directed by

theory. He was open to any chance. In a harsh moment Lavoisier wrote that his rival's work formed "a web of experiments uninterrupted by reasoning."

Research in "natural philosophy", Priestley thought, was like hunting. Hunters who went out and beat the bushes most energetically did not always succeed. A passerby might bag the game.

Very big game awaited him.

Like Lavoisier and other researchers, Priestley heated his chemicals by means of a "burning glass." A "burning glass" was a convex lens which converged the sun's rays at a focal point where the sample to be heated could be placed. Lord Shelburne furnished Priestley with a lens larger than he had ever been able to afford.

A burning glass produces the most heat in brilliant sunlight and England's skies are often gray. It was on an unusually hot, bright Sunday in August of 1774 that Priestley — who had spent his boyhood Sabbaths in church and in Old Hall reading, writing and praying — saw his chance for a new experiment.

He focused his lens upon a sample of red oxide of mercury.

To his surprise and bewilderment, the heated oxide gave off a large quantity of gas. Since this gas did not dissolve in water, it could not be the carbon dioxide which he had expected. What was more bewildering, a candle placed in a container of this new gas burned with a truly dazzling flame.

Priestley was afraid that his sample of red oxide of mercury was impure. He tried his experiment again and again. Each time he got the same result.

Eight months after that first exciting Sunday morning he announced his discovery to the president of the Royal Society. A believer in phlogiston, the old "spirit of fire", he called his new gas "dephlogisticated air." Lavoisier and the scientific world would call it oxygen.

No matter what the name, Joseph Priestley had discovered the gas which is the most abundant element in the Earth's crust and constitutes one-fifth of all its atmosphere, the gas without which life as we know it could not exist.

On a European tour with Lord Shelburne, Priestley was invited to dinner at the Lavoisiers' small chateau. There he described in bold, though stammering, French his recent experiments. Lavoisier would quickly repeat and confirm the work in his own splendid laboratory, not always giving credit to his visitor.

Idling in Paris was no pleasure for Priestley. He thought the buildings magnificent but the streets foul and dirty. Learned Parisians told him that he was the only scientist they had ever met who believed in God. Gratefully he returned to Calme and his family. There he could think and write beside the fire with his wife and children around him. He could enjoy daily chess and backgammon with Mary and whist and other non-gambling card games with his children.

He organized his time strictly, making endless schedules for himself, calculating even the hours he meant to devote to each new book. For exercise he took long, brisk walks. Vigorous athletics dulled the mind, he thought, but walking was both healthful and delightful. He never owned a horse or carriage.

Gradually, however, life at Calme began to be less pleasant. Lord Shelburne grew unfriendly.

It was true that, in addition to scientific papers, Priestley had recently published his major religious work, *Disquisitions Relating to Matter and Spirit*. Man and the universe are all matter, he had declared. There is no spirit apart from matter, there is no separate soul. God is the "intelligent first cause." He brings about all good and all evil. What men call evil is, in fact, a part of God's grand design. That design will at last bring a reign of peace and love on earth.

The anger aroused throughout England by the *Disquisitions* was, Priestley himself said, "such as hardly could be imagined." Lord Shelburne had political ambitions. Perhaps he thought that continued sponsorship of his "heretic librarian" would be a disadvantage to him.

At all events, Priestley felt his sponsor's coldness and decided to leave Calme.

In 1780 he and his family moved to Birmingham. There he became minister at the New Meeting House, perhaps the most liberal church in England. In the bustling industrial city he was to spend the happiest ten years of his life.

Many dissenters lived in Birmingham. As always, Priestley especially liked the young people and spent much time instructing them.

Hints came that the government might offer him a pension to finance his scientific work but he refused. He thought the government corrupt. He preferred accepting help from Mary's prosperous brothers and other men who were true "lovers of liberty", "lovers of science."

He built up a splendid library and helped set up one for the city as well. He was also able to build and equip a fine two-story laboratory, separated from Mary's clean and orderly household.

When his children and their friends pursued him there, he amused them with magic lantern pictures and light shocks from his electric machine. If the young visitors asked to use his air gun he let them use his wig, set on a pedestal, for target practice.

He preached an eloquent anti-slavery sermon. He found good companions at the Lunar Society, a brilliant group which included James Watt, inventor of the steam engine, and Erasmus Darwin, grandfather of Charles Darwin.

He entertained at his own table Quakers, Catholics, clergymen of the Church of England and others. He would no doubt have welcomed Muslims and Buddhists if any had been available in Birmingham.

But once again, shadows were beginning to gather.

Priestley had always advocated independence for the American colonies. Now, in the 1780's, not seeing the horrors to come, he wholeheartedly praised the French Revolution.

Much of England was terrified. The Americans had won their freedom but they were a wide ocean away. France was just across the English Channel.

The revolutionists beheaded their king, then moved on to further violence. In 1790, a French mob stormed the grim old Parisian prison, the Bastille, and set the prisoners free.

On the first anniversary of Bastille Day, an English mob stormed the city of Birmingham. Unlike the French, their cry was "King and Church."

Joseph Priestley with his many writings on freedom of thought was a prime target for the mob's fear and anger. The rumor spread — though it was untrue — that he had helped to organize a Bastille Day celebration in the city. In the eyes of the mob, he was a seditious revolutionary who would destroy religion and the state.

Priestley and Mary were playing backgammon in the firelight of their home, Fair Hill, when a messenger brought word that the mob had burned down the New Meeting House. The mob was now moving toward Fair Hill. The young men of his congregation volunteered to defend their minister's home but he refused to let them try.

A carriage whisked him and his wife to a friend's home. Left behind, Fair Hill was attacked and vandalized. Hot coals brought from a tavern across the fields set the fine building ablaze.

Priestley himself was in danger. He refused a disguise but set out on a confused and lengthy ride on horseback and by coach to London. There, his host demanded that for his own safety he wear women's clothes when he went outdoors. Members of the Royal Society turned their backs on him.

The Birmingham riots ended after three days as the government sent troops to calm the city, but life in England was no longer secure for Priestley. His sons, now young men, were blackened by their father's reputation and could not find suitable work. France offered him citizenship and a place in the Convention which would draw up a new constitution. But, though a champion of liberty and the Revolution, Priestley realized that he did not know France well, and he spoke only a self-taught, stammering French.

Numbers of Englishmen who found their own government repressive were going to America. Soon, all three of the Priestley sons sailed for the New World. Priestley and his wife followed. They boarded the sailing vessel Samson in early April of 1794. While the refugees were at sea, Lavoisier lost his head to the guillotine. The news could not reach the storm-tossed vessel.

The Atlantic crossing lasted two months. Joseph, Jr. met his parents in New York. Soon, the Priestley sons, with a few friends, journeyed to Northumberland, a village five days' journey up the Susquehanna River from Philadelphia. There they bought farmland and hoped to found a colony of Jacobins, as friends of France were called.

Even in the New World, dreams could fail. Northumberland was not, after all, to become a community of English liberals. The difficulties of organizing a large settlement were too great.

But again, the Priestleys followed their sons. Mary could

not forget the terrors of the Birmingham riots and was afraid of cities. Life in the Pennsylvania countryside might sometimes be lonely but it would be inexpensive and safe.

In Northumberland Priestley threw away his wig and stopped powdering his hair. He helped his youngest son, Harry, tend his new farm. Mary designed a pleasant two-story house on a green hillside overlooking the river. She died before the house was finished but her husband settled there in 1796. Once again, he set about gathering laboratory equipment and collecting books — four thousand of them.

For fresh ideas and good conversation, he went regularly to Philadelphia. His good friend Benjamin Franklin was dead but the Philosophical Society, which Franklin had founded, welcomed him. The Unitarian Church invited him to preach. George Washington received him. He came to know John Adams and the fiery young Thomas Jefferson.

Still, he had not left enemies behind. He was pursued by Peter Porcupine, a scandal-mongering journalist. That "political caterpillar", as one indignant editor called him, discovered letters written to Priestley by a friend who praised the French for their military adventures all over Europe. Peter Porcupine accused Priestley of being a French spy and demanded he be deported.

The threat was real under the Alien and Sedition Law of 1798 which severely restricted free speech, but Priestley had, as usual, no intention of remaining silent. The Constitution of the United States was the best that had ever been devised by man, he wrote. Nevertheless it had flaws which he would continue to point out.

Fortunately, the Alien and Sedition Law expired in 1800, the year that Priestley, ever thirsty for new knowledge, decided to learn Chinese! Thomas Jefferson, his loyal friend and ardent admirer, became President. Priestley could live out his last years under the kind of government for which he had always longed.

In this New World he never lost his enthusiasm for his laboratory. He continued to publish, still defending phlogiston, that imaginary "spirit of fire" which Lavoisier and his own research had by now disproved. He continued also his previous work on the deadly gas carbon monoxide which "is inflammable and essentially different from all other oxyds."

The old dissenting minister saw no conflict between science and religion. Both were parts of one unified creation moving always toward the good.

He died on a winter morning in 1804. He had visited his laboratory only two days before and had just finished proof-reading a pamphlet which compared Jesus and Socrates.

Benjamin Franklin called his friend a "diligent experimenter and furious free thinker." Over the years Priestley was called by many names: honest heretic, seditious revolutionary, canker worm of England's happiness, one of the few lives precious to mankind, proud and haughty scorner, comet in the system, Gunpowder Priestley.

He himself wrote of his life, "I saw reason to embrace what is generally called the heterodox side of almost every question."

Seventy years after his death, on the porch of Priestley's Northumberland home plans were made for organization of the American Chemical Society. The old rebel was respectable at last.

Chapter III
John Dalton
Quaker Atomist

The village schoolmaster was having a hard day. His pupils refused to do their lessons. When, in desperation, he locked the door upon them, they smashed the schoolhouse windows and climbed out to freedom.

Nobody in the tiny Cumberland village of Eaglesfield could well blame John Dalton, the schoolmaster. He was, after all, only twelve years old.

Nobody, including John himself, seems to have been sure of the exact date of his birth. The Daltons were Quakers. As dissenters from England's established church, their names were not entered in the official parish register. The Quakers kept their own records of births. But somehow John didn't make the list even though his brother Jonathan and his sister Mary did. Perhaps his less than careful father simply forgot to report the new arrival. Years later friends and relatives decided that the birth date must have been September 5th or 6th, 1766.

The Dalton home was a thatched roof row cottage of only two rooms. Although the family had hearty oats, turnips, beets and potatoes to keep them from hunger, life was stark. The only beauty was supplied by a view of neighboring hills and that nearby "pocket of Switzerland," England's Lake district, with its lovely peaks and valleys and its deep blue waters.

As a boy John helped his father weave coarse gray

Cumberland woolen, the clack-clack of the loom filling his ears. In summer he was kept busy on the family farm.

Luckily, in a country where only one out of 215 people could read, Quakers were dedicated to education for their sons and daughters. John was sent early to Eaglesfield's Pardshaw Hall and there he met a sympathetic teacher. John Fletcher did not force the classics upon the little boy who was obviously fascinated with numbers. Fletcher offered instead "mensuration, surveying, navigation and so forth." Latin and Greek could wait. The King's English could wait, too. John Dalton would never lose his broad Cumbrian dialect or his forthright manner of speaking and writing.

He remained at school until he was eleven years old. At twelve he became a teacher himself in charge of all ages from toddlers to rambunctious teens. The teens regularly challenged him to very un-Quakerish battles in the local graveyard.

When he was fifteen John left the village to seek his fortune. With his parents' blessing he set out on foot, so legend reports, a bundle of clothing in one hand, in the other hand that newly-fashionable piece of gentleman's gear, an umbrella. His immediate goal, forty-five miles distant, was Kendal, a market town and weaving center with a population of 5,000. A metropolis!

In Kendal John joined his brother Jonathan as an under-teacher at a Quaker school larger and better equipped than Pardshaw Hall. Soon the two teenagers were themselves schoolmasters known for their country manners and stern discipline. Meantime, John himself was learning.

In Eaglesfield he had been encouraged by a kindly Quaker named Elihu Robinson. Robinson was an amateur meteorologist, a maker of sundials, the organizer of a local book club and a correspondent of Benjamin Franklin. Robinson had shared readings with John and given him instruction in mathematics and "natural philosophy," the eighteenth century name for science.

In Kendal he found an even more remarkable friend and teacher, the blind thinker John Gough.

John Gough at thirty was a master of Latin, Greek and French. Blind since the age of two, he had never learned to write but he could do a wide range of mathematical and physical problems in his head. He kept a meteorological journal and could tell by touch, taste and smell the plants for twenty miles around Kendal.

All these matters fascinated John Dalton. He began his own meteorological journal, "Observations Upon the Weather." He would keep that journal daily for 57 years. He learned to make his own thermometers, marvelling that "men and other animals" maintain the same bodily heat in Siberia as in "the burning sands of Africa." He also collected flowers, butterflies and flies, studied caterpillars, maggots, mice and snails. He even weighed his own food intake and excretions.

In addition, he read all the scientific books he could find and popular magazines as well. "The Gentleman's Diary" and "The Lady's Diary" regularly proposed problems in science and mathematics. John's solutions won several prizes. Occasionally he tried his hand at solving ethical problems. "Did a benefactor or the person receiving help get more pleasure?" the Diary asked. Common-sensical John thought the benefactor was the happier. He himself was too poor to have any illusions about the joys of an empty pocket.

Poverty continued to dog him through his twelve poorly-paid years of teaching at Kendal. To supplement his small salary he sold mounted specimens of plants gathered on long walks through the Lake district. Though he still earned little money, his walks wakened in him endless questions about fogs and clouds, winds and storms, rains and vapors.

Gradually the narrowness of his world began to press hard upon him. Unpolished and ill-educated, he nevertheless sensed in himself great powers.

In 1790 he wrote to Elihu Robinson, his Eaglesfield friend, and to his uncle Thomas Greenup, announcing that he wanted to study medicine or law. Robinson replied that he would probably make a good doctor but that he was clearly gifted in "that noble labor of teaching youth." Uncle Thomas answered more bluntly that medical or legal education was "totally out of reach" of a young man without any money.

Dalton refused to be discouraged. He continued his scientific reading and experimentation. In the late 18th century one clever man could master most of the proven body of scientific knowledge, and Dalton seems to have had no doubt of his own capacity. He decided to offer, for the sum of 5 shillings, a series of 13 lectures with demonstrations covering "optics, mechanics, pneumatics, astronomy, the use of globes and fire."

Scientific lectures were popular at the time but, alas, after the first sessions the youthful scholar addressed mostly empty seats. Eloquence was not one of his natural gifts. Still he kept stubbornly on, presenting his series in several nearby towns.

He also set about writing his first book which was to have the forthright title *Meteorological Observations and Essays*. He hoped in his book to "illustrate and exemplify the Principles and a few Practical rules for judging of the weather deduced from experience." The rules would be useful for "husbandman and mariner" as well as for the general public.

In his *Observations* Dalton wrote about the barometer, thermometer, hydrometer and rain gauge, all instruments he had himself constructed to measure air pressure, temperature, water vapor and rain fall. He discussed the aurora borealis, that shimmering display of colors which often lit up the Lake district sky. He explained evaporation. He described how he had determined the temperature at which water becomes dew using only a thermometer, "a clean, dry tumbler" and the flow of a mountain stream.

Now, borrowing time from his studies, he took his first trip to London to attend a national Quaker meeting. The city with its noise and bustle and especially its many taxis or hacks he found well worth visiting "at least once."

Soon city life was to claim him. New College of Manchester was looking for a teacher of "mathematics, theoretic and experimental natural philosophy and chemistry." John Gough recommended his young friend.

The twenty-seven-year old Dalton who set out from Kendal in 1793 was near-sighted and wore spectacles, but he had no difficulty seeing what he wanted to see and could read and study endlessly. He had a broad brow, a substantial nose and a strong jutting chin. No man to push other people about, he was not going to be pushed himself.

New College of Manchester was a Unitarian-sponsored school. The staff of dissenter instructors was small but capable. Traveling lecturers brought the latest knowledge. Manchester itself was a city alive with new manufactures and mushrooming fortunes. It did not yet have a university but it had an excellent free library. Dalton lived first at "large and elegant" New College. His third story room was light and airy, had two windows and a cheery fireplace. As a philosopher he liked living 10 yards above the ground.

His teaching skills were mellowing. He was using Antoine Lavoisier's *Traité Elementaire de la Chimie* as a chemistry textbook and his students liked him. But he was restless still. After six years, sure that he could attract private pupils and eager to have more time for his own research, he left New College. He would teach privately in

Manchester for the rest of his working life. He counted among his students James Joule, the physicist who was to give his name to units of heat.

For nearly thirty years Dalton boarded at the home of William Johns, a Unitarian minister. In that tolerant household he could withdraw into his own thoughts or suddenly propel a scientific question into the midst of the general chatter. He seldom spoke about religion, Catherine Johns remembered, though he lived by the six Quaker "testimonies" — plain and exact speech, refusal to take an oath, refusal to doff his hat, plain clothing, non-violence and exclusion of the arts. He made an exception for music which he loved and tried unsuccessfully to introduce into Quaker services.

Though his life style was plain, Dalton was no grim-faced Scrooge. He enjoyed the learned visitors who came to the Johns' fireside and regularly smoked a late evening pipe with his host. Every Thursday afternoon he walked to the "Dog and Partridge" pub for a game of lawn bowls. Now and again he took brief trips back to Eaglesfield and Kendal and to his beloved Lake district.

The center of John Dalton's life, however, lay just across Manchester's George Street at the Literary and Philosophical Society. In 1794 only a year after his arrival in Manchester he was invited to join the "Lit and Phil." He soon became an officer and would be president for 25 years. There he was given a laboratory where he could teach and perform scientific experiments. He went to the laboratory so promptly each morning that a neighbor declared she could set her clock by the moment Dr. Dalton opened his window to read his thermometer.

Just four weeks after joining the "Lit and Phil" he boldly presented his first paper on a surprising subject, "Extraordinary Facts Relating to the Vision of Colors: With

Observations by Mr. John Dalton." The paper was the first serious study anyone had ever done of what we now call "color blindness."

Dalton himself had "red blindness" or protanopia. He had once given his mother a pair of scarlet silk stockings which she admired but would not wear to Quaker meeting since they were so brilliant in hue. Dalton himself thought them drab and decided that the old lady was losing her vision. It was a geranium flower which alerted him to his own problem. His friends called the flower pink but to him in daylight it appeared sky blue, by candle light yet another shade.

A careful check showed him that except for his brother Jonathan nobody he knew saw colors as he did. Experimenting in his usual careful way, he discovered that in a darkened room when a ray of sunlight was passed through a glass prism most people saw a fan of six bright colors: red, orange, yellow, green, blue and purple. He saw clearly only two; yellow and blue with a hint of purple. To study this curious phenomenon he soon gathered together ribbons of different colors and composed a set of questions. He sent these along with a prism to a Merryport family whose members had a problem like his own. He assembled meticulous data from twenty such color blind persons, as usual using the simplest of means. It was on these findings that his paper was based.

That paper so impressed the "Lit and Phil" that they published it in their "Memoirs." It would inspire decades of investigation.

In all Dalton would present well over a hundred papers to his colleagues in the "Lit and Phil." Some fifty of these were published in the "Memoirs." Among these many, the most memorable was one which he presented in 1803.

John Dalton was about to make his greatest contribution to science: the chemical atomic theory.

Dalton's idea, though startling to his contemporaries, was not entirely new.

Long ago an aristocratic young philosopher named Heraclitus had decided that Leucippus, his fellow Greek, was right. Matter was not "continuous" as was believed by almost everybody of the time, and, as it turned out, nearly everybody for the next 2,000 years. A raindrop, said Heraclitus, could not be forever divided into smaller and smaller portions nor could a chip of marble nor any other object. Invisible to the eye but at the heart of all matter were tiny particles which could not be divided. Heraclitus chose to call them "atomos" — in Greek, uncut.

The great Aristotle pooh-poohed the idea. The philosopher Plato said Heraclitus' writings should be banned. Nobody had, after all, any way of testing or seeing atoms. Besides, the Greeks didn't believe in experiment. If some genie-of-the-future had magically dropped a twentieth century scanning, tunnelling electron microscope on the heights of the Acropolis, the Greeks would have ignored it.

For two millennia occasional rebel thinkers in the Western world toyed with the idea of individual, indivisible particles. No one, not even Isaac Newton, discoverer of gravity, had got very far with such speculations.

It was John Dalton who was now to declare the theory of matter for which, all unknowingly, the scientific world had been waiting. For years Dalton had been investigating the diffusion of gases, the solubility of some elements in others, the mystery of the earth's atmosphere. Despite a stubborn self-reliance which sometimes made him deaf to the ideas of other scientists, he had read extensively in the scientific literature and he knew about the work of Lavoisier and other contemporaries.

How to put together the findings of so many researchers including Priestley's discovery of oxygen, Lavoisier's work on combustion and the chemical elements as well as his own painstaking investigations? How come up with a coherent theory of matter? The pieces of the puzzle were fitting together in Dalton's mind. The solution appeared simple which did not surprise him. For Dalton the simplest explanation of a phenomenon was bound to be the truest. His ideas could be easily stated.

All elements, he now declared, are made up of tiny indivisible particles. These particles, following Heraclitus, he called "atoms."

All atoms of a given element are chemically identical. In chemical reactions, every atom of gold is like every other atom of gold. Gold is gold, silver is silver, lead is lead.

What is more, atoms cannot be destroyed or created during chemical reactions, although the atoms of different elements may combine to form compounds. The gases hydrogen and oxygen in combination, for instance, form water. Hydrogen and nitrogen form ammonia.

The chemical reaction forming a compound does not involve a change in the atoms. It involves a change in the way in which atoms are combined. Atoms of different elements combine to form compounds in fixed, small, whole number mass ratios. Atoms of the same elements in different proportions may also form more than one compound with a definite whole number mass and atomic ratio for each compound. There are no fractions in Dalton's atomic theory.

Not all the details of Dalton's work are accepted today. He had not, after all, any way of determining the actual mass or weight of atoms. He did calculate relative weights. Some of his calculations have turned out to be wrong, largely because he thought a water molecule contains one atom of hydrogen to each atom of oxygen when, in fact, it contains two. And he was wrong about the indestructibility of atoms. They can be "smashed" as the cyclotron and the atom bomb have proved.

Yet Dalton's atomic theory stands as a revolutionary achievement. Over time, it has led to a vast number of experiments. The proof of a great scientific idea is not that it is right in minute detail but that it opens doors to fresh discoveries and greater understandings. Today, every beginning chemistry student encounters and accepts the basic idea of matter proposed by the quiet man from Eaglesfield.

As the years went by, Dalton enthusiastically continued his scientific explorations. His apparatus might have seemed meager to Lavoisier in that great laboratory in Paris, but he had far finer equipment than the homemade gauges and "good clean tumblers" of his youth. He was a notable citizen of Manchester now and received many distinguished visitors and many honors. He was elected a member of the French Academy of Science and a Fellow of the English Royal Society. In 1826 he received the first Royal Medal "for the development of the chemical theory of definite proportions, usually called the atomic theory, and for his various other labors and discoveries in physical and chemical science." He was invited to be part of an expedition to the Polar region, an invitation he refused since he did not want to leave his laboratory.

Always he remained himself. When he was presented at King William's court he refused to wear the elegant clothing and carry the sword customary at such occasions. Instead, he wore the scarlet robe he had received as an honoree of Oxford University, apparently never guessing how he stood out, a red bird among King William's courtiers.

When the King asked him how he was getting on in Manchester, he replied, "just middlin', I think." A friend later suggested that this was no reply to make to a King. Dalton asked in broad Cumbrian dialect what else he could say to "sic like fowk."

John Dalton never married. He gave a comical account of one lovely Quaker lady of Manchester who asked him for dinner. He accepted the invitation, thinking himself in no danger from her charms. Surely such a beautiful woman would not also be intelligent. Alas, his hostess began to talk of English grammar, the merits of different dictionaries, the use of "dephlogisticated Marine acid in bleaching" and the effects of opium on the animal system! Dalton lost his heart and his appetite for a full week but he managed to recover and returned to his bachelor ways.

Catherine Johns believed he enjoyed the company of her witty sister. He had warm friendships with other ladies. But as a young man he must have felt that he could not support a wife and children on a schoolmaster's meager pay. The older and more prosperous Dalton was wedded to his science and his ordered life. Besides, he had strong views on how to take care of himself. For colds, he heated his own mixture of licorice, vinegar and molasses in a laboratory pipkin and was sure he got good results from this inexpensive "simple." When one of his doctors claimed that a prescribed medicine had caused Dalton's recovery from an illness, the patient replied that this was very strange. He had not taken the medicine; he had wanted to analyze it first.

He remained a warm friend and brother, appreciative of those who, like the blind John Gough, had helped him. In his original will he left a sum of money to set up a Professorship in Atomic Theory at Oxford University. He later changed the bequest, leaving the money instead to his friends, the Johns family, who had fallen on hard times.

Dalton's last home on Faulkner Street was no mansion by Manchester standards, but damask draperies hung at the windows and engraved portraits of famous men decorated the walls. Cut glass pieces — dinner, breakfast and tea services—stood on the cupboard shelves. A large mahogany bookcase held a library of some 700 rare volumes. One hundred and twenty ounces of silver and a valuable collection of dried plants were his other treasures.

On the last full day of his life Dalton recorded in a trembling hand his customary meteorological observation. He had made some 200,000 such observations in his life. Today he wrote simply "little rain." On the next morning, July 27, 1844, he died.

Antoine Lavoisier, son and heir of a wealthy lawyer, educated in the finest schools of France, had been guillotined, his headless body tossed into a common grave. The body of John Dalton, self-educated son of a poor village weaver, was laid out in Manchester Town Hall. Forty-thousand admirers came to pay their respect. He was carried to a resting place in Ardwick Cemetery in a splendid procession of nearly a hundred carriages. Shops and warehouses were closed in his honor.

Yet violence would at last touch this gentle Quaker. His laboratory at the Literary and Philosophical Society along with the bulk of his letters and papers were destroyed in the 1940 bombing of Manchester during World War II.

His renown did not die in the flames.

Harold Urey, a twentieth century scientific giant, would say of John Dalton's work, "It is my belief that the discovery of atoms and molecules will remain for all time as the most fundamental work of chemistry."

Chapter IV
Jöns Jacob Berzelius
Traveler on Bridges to the Truth

One day in 1796, the principal of Linköping High School lifted the pen from the inkwell on his desk and grimly applied it to the paper before him. Jöns Jacob Berzelius, the principal wrote, was "a youth of good natural parts but bad habits and dubious prospects." He had missed sixty-three class hours during the previous term.

It was a harsh report on an orphaned teen-ager who had put himself through high school by tutoring and doing farm work, harvesting hay, cutting turnips, chopping wood and building mouse traps. During one long Swedish winter, the boy's home had been a storage shed kept only warm enough to prevent his roommates, the potatoes, from freezing. Meantime, he had competed for food with seven children at the home of a drunken farm-wife.

But Jacob Berzelius was not only poor. He was also self-confident and rebellious. He showed little enthusiasm for Latin and Greek, downright refused to study Hebrew and was often absent from the school's morning prayers. He preferred spending his mornings in the countryside with butterfly net and shotgun.

Net and gun were natural enough possessions for a country boy who boasted of having collected specimen of three hundred and sixty-nine insects, "many of them rare," and who was expert at shooting and mounting birds. Students at Linköping High School were, however, forbidden to own firearms. When a shot was accidently fired in Berzelius' room, the principal decided to whip and expel his disobedient pupil.

He had not set himself an easy task. Jacob Berzelius was a sturdy boy with broad shoulders, bright irreverent eyes, a strong jutting nose and an impudent dimple in his rounded chin. He did not appear at the time set for the whipping. Meanwhile, the Bishop of Linköping, an inspector at the high school, had intervened on his behalf. Despite a poor record, the boy had some talent, the Bishop declared. He also came of a worthy family.

Berzelius had been born in 1779 in Vaversunda, Östergötland. His father, a Lutheran pastor and teacher, died when the boy was four years old. His mother soon remarried. Her new husband was Anders Eckmarck, also a school teacher and Lutheran pastor.

Pastor Eckmarck was a good man, eager to share his love of learning, especially of natural history. But he found himself with a modest income and a family of seven children, five from a previous marriage plus Jacob and the boy's little sister.

Five years after this marriage, the mother died. Pastor Eckmarck took a third wife, and Berzelius was sent back to Vaversunda to live with an uncle. In that quarrelsome family there were also seven children. There was also a drunken, no doubt over-worked mother who did not welcome the newcomer. At fourteen, Berzelius escaped to High School in Linköping, a quiet old town settled since the Bronze age.

Berzelius' mother had hoped that he would become a clergyman like his father, grandfathers and great-grandfathers. His early diaries, begun when he was six years old, had often spoken of God and the hope that the Lord would help him to be a better person. But his heart was not in the pulpit. His true gift was for the natural world. At the age of fifteen while still a High School student, he decided to become a physician. In that work he might hope to earn a reasonable livelihood. Perhaps more important, as a medical student he could study science.

In 1796, carrying with him little more than his Bishop's recommendation and his school principal's grudging letter of introduction, he set out for the University of Uppsala.

Poised on Europe's northern rim, the three hundred year old University was the traditional center of Swedish culture. There the students were divided into "nations" representing the different Swedish provinces. The "nations" gave students practical help and a social life.

No hermit, Berzelius would always be happy among good friends. He liked laughter and comic stories. But his life was not a comedy. His merriment was often interrupted by serious migraine headaches and he was still poor.

Uppsala medical training began with physics and chemistry. Berzelius did brilliant work in physics, but he could not afford to pay the fees charged by the chemistry lecturer. That science he set out to teach himself by reading recent German texts. Overall his academic record was not impressive, and he battled often with his professors.

A watercolor portrait of the period shows a thin, earnest young man, dressed in plain jacket and knee britches. The portrait has been called "The Hungry Berzelius."

Hunger did not dull Berzelius' self-confidence or his combativeness. Since the university laboratory gave him little chance to work, he set up a make-shift laboratory in the windowless closet of his own rented room. Soon he worked out a new method for producing laughing gas, and he produced oxygen. Oxygen had been discovered thirty years before by Priestley and independently by Carl Scheele, a Swedish pharmacist, but the new gas, or "fire air," still seemed miraculous. When a glowing stick which Berzelius dipped into the oxygen caught fire and lit up the walls of his tiny laboratory, he was filled with "a pure inner delight."

More marvels lay ahead. In 1800, the Italian physicist, Alessandro Volta, invented the Voltaic pile, the father of today's batteries, which produced an electric current by means of chemical reaction.

Two English scientists promptly discovered that the new "galvanic current" could separate water into its two component elements, hydrogen and oxygen. The pile was demonstrated in Stockholm and an impromptu Galvanic Society was formed.

In excitement, Berzelius constructed an inexpensive pile of his own. He alternated a series of sixty zinc washers with sixty polished copper coins.

With the help of his step-brother, Christopher Eckmarck, also a science student at Uppsala, he used his pile to investigate various organic substances. Researchers all over Europe were currently exploring the differences between organic and inorganic substances. Organic chemicals had been first defined as chemicals produced by plants and animals. Now they were beginning to be defined as any substances which contain carbon, an element which is a vital ingredient of living things. Organic substances are far more numerous than mineral, or inorganic, but they are also far more difficult to analyze.

Berzelius was playing a fascinating game. In the summer of 1800, he took his Voltaic pile to Medevi, a spa owned by the royal physician, Sven Anders Hedin. Nineteenth century Europeans flocked to spas in the belief that mineral waters could cure illnesses from ulcers and paralysis to St. Vitus's Dance.

Berzelius analyzed the contents of the Medevi mineral waters. He also tried the galvanic current on his patients. To his disappointment, only one patient seemed to be helped. But his experiments became the subject of a dissertation which he presented to the university in 1802.

Despite his stormy academic career, his Medevi thesis was accepted. The M.D. degree was granted and Berzelius went as a government physician to several small islands in Lake Malaren near Stockholm.

Luckily the royal physician, Hedin, recognized that, though the young doctor was sincere enough, his heart was in the laboratory, not at the bedside.

With Hedin's recommendation, Berzelius received an appointment as assistant to the professor of medicine and pharmacy at the School of Surgery in Stockholm. Since the School of Surgery paid him nothing, he also became a government doctor to the Stockholm poor. His salary made him only a little richer than his patients who, he found, were obliged to live on a diet of cabbage, lettuce, nettles and asparagus. He took his own scanty meals with Dr. Lars Werner, owner of a garden spa. There, Dr. Werner hoped to dose his patients with the artificial mineral waters which Berzelius would create.

The spa, alas, went bankrupt. Berzelius, always generous, had signed papers which made him financially responsible. It would take him ten years to repay the debt. He would never be a good businessman.

But he was still undaunted. He had made a new and important friend, the rich mine owner, Wilhelm Hissinger, who shared his passion for research and taught him mineralogy. He went to live in an old Stockholm building known as "the German baker's house", owned by Hissinger. There the two set up their private laboratory.

They soon reported experiments proving that the decomposition of water achieved by the English scientists was not unique. A galvanic current could separate the components of most salts dissolved in water. Acids would move to one pole of the battery, alkalis, or bases, to the other.

Hissinger showed Berzelius a sample of the rare metal known as bastnas or tungsten. The two men did independent analyses of the tungsten and agreed that they had found in it a new element which they called cerium.

The discovery caused a great controversy, but Berzelius, stubbornly and rightly, held to his claim. He would later discover also the elements silicon, selenium and thorium.

In 1807, when he was twenty-eight years old, he was appointed professor of medicine and pharmacy at the Stockholm School of Surgery, soon to be reorganized as the independent Caroline Institute. Now he could give up his work as a charity doctor and devote himself to research. The eight-by-six meter teaching laboratory had unvented fireplaces. Doors and windows had to be left open for the escape of smoke and fumes. A coal fire had always to be kept burning by Anna, the stern and trustworthy housekeeper. But the government paid for the coal and the laboratory equipment and glassware. No other laboratory in Sweden was as well supported. "Turd cooking," the countryman Berzelius happily called his experiments.

He was still far from rich but life was full. He had laboratory space for ten students. Gifted young men came to study with him from Sweden and abroad. He also taught at the War Academy. Sweden had recently lost a disastrous war with Russia. Countless young men had died, not of wounds but of infectious diseases. The government was eager to train better medical officers.

Berzelius soon realized that he knew little about physiology. The truth was that nobody had the answers to many questions about animal chemistry.

Berzelius set out to solve the mysteries himself. He presented the results of his new experiments in his published lectures on animal chemistry and in his great textbook on general chemistry.

In ten years he would set a record no other chemist has ever equalled. He would analyze some two thousand chemical compounds and mixtures, organic and inorganic. Using oxygen as the basic measure, he would determine with surprising accuracy the components and the atomic weights. Of the forty-nine elements known when his work began, he and his students would determine the atomic weight of forty-five.

Trusted assistants were allowed to do calculations. Berzelius himself did most of the experiments. He was by now a skilled glass-blower. He improved the blow pipe, that standard experimental tool which produces a jet of fire by forcing a mixture of flammable gas and air, or oxygen, through a small nozzle at high pressure. Later, when he was famous, he would carry a blow pipe like a magic wand in the pocket of his dinner jacket and use it to amuse and startle duchesses and princesses.

But equipment was serious business, not a parlor trick, in these busy early years. Berzelius was the first experimentalist to use tubing made of rubber, that tough and flexible new material from far-off South America, which chemists were just beginning to make available. He was the first to use filter paper which sifted out solid particles from liquids and gases. He was the first to use the desiccator, a tightly-lidded glass vessel in which substances could be dried or other "hygroscopic" water-absorbing substances could be prevented from taking up moisture. To these tools, Berzelius added his steady hands, a strong sense of taste, smell and sight and a memory so keen that he did not have to label his bottled chemicals. Above all, he had his ever-active brain and his dedication.

Berzelius believed passionately in the importance of

experimentation. Theories were "bridges to the truth," but every theory must be tested and ruthlessly discarded if it could not be proven in the laboratory.

"We must put the right questions to Nature and wait patiently for the answers," he said. "One may shine like the sun and be extinguished by a candle snuffer." "The wings of hypothesis" may melt like wax.

Though possessed of experimental gifts Berzelius held strongly to certain important theories. His championship of Dalton's theory of the atom played a large part in winning acceptance of that theory among chemists.

Neither Dalton nor Berzelius could know, of course, that their "indivisible" atom was, in fact, divisible. A false theory at a certain period in the development of a science may "serve the purpose as well as a true one," said Berzelius.

Berzelius also championed the law of definite proportions. He was certain that the Creator of the world was a reliable mathematician. Elements do not combine to form compounds in a haphazard fashion, like pennies thrown into a wishing well. They combine in certain fixed and quite simple mathematical proportions. Specific elements can be trusted always to combine in specific ways. "Stoichiometry" or the law of definite proportions makes possible accurate chemical analysis.

There remained a further question. Elements can combine in definite proportions to form compounds. Yes. But what holds these elements so tightly together that no physical force can separate them? Why don't the different elements fly apart or simply mix like sugar water? Many mixtures do exist. Why do compounds — water itself, for instance, the most important compound on earth — occur at all?

For Berzelius the answer came from the new science of electrochemistry which he himself helped to found. All atoms carry an electric charge, he decided. There are two kinds of electricity. Some atoms are electrically positive, others are electrically negative. Opposite charges attract. When substances in the correct proportion meet, a chemical reaction takes place and a compound, a wholly new substance held together by electrical charges, is formed. Berzelius would insist on his "dualistic theory" all his life.

The human body, he thought, was a chemical workshop made up of reactions between many compounds. True, it held mysteries which might never be solved. The human brain, which could calculate the motion of far-off worlds, might never be able to understand itself fully. But animal research should go on despite experimental difficulties. His own analysis of body fluids, haemoglobin, muscles, bone marrow and tissues from the eye was not easy. Papers on certain body fluids were never likely to be best sellers, he admitted wryly.

With all his enthusiasm minerals gradually enticed him away from study of living bodies. Mining was an important industry in Sweden. Both Berzelius' collaborator Hissinger and his friend, Johan Gahn, a mineralogist and mining expert, encouraged him to turn to work in this field.

In mineralogy, Berzelius found himself at the center of a new storm. Mineralogy of the time was a descriptive science. Naturalists recorded what could be seen: color, shape, cleavage patterns, crystal structure. Berzelius set out to study what could not be seen: the chemical components of minerals and the resulting chemical reactions.

Naturalists resented his slicing, dissolving and otherwise invading their precious samples, but, as always, Berzelius stood firm. To description he would add an understanding of chemical process. He created a classification system for minerals based on chemical contents. The new system was at first rejected as an absurdity but it would, in time, win him

England's Copley Medal. It is largely in use today.

He also invented a practical sign language for chemists. Lavoisier had given the elements a standard set of names. But names grew long and awkward. A language studded with micropolysacharides, trinitrobenzenes and prostaglandins would be as forbidding as Chinese or Arabic. The old symbols of the alchemists were much too fanciful and appeared in no printer's fonts.

Berzelius proposed that for chemists everywhere each element be represented by the first letter of its Latin or, in a few cases, Greek name. When two elements began with the same letter, two letters would be used. H would stand for hydrogen, for instance. He for helium. C would stand for carbon. Cl for chlorine. Subscripts would show the quantities in which the different elements appeared in compounds. By the end of the twentieth century, scientists would recognize more than twice the number of elements which Berzelius first knew. With so many additions Berzelius' simple system still works.

The hardworking decade from 1807 to 1817 brought the young chemist wide-spread fame but it damaged his health. Suddenly he had no energy, no wish or strength to work. Medicines did not help him. His alarmed friends decided upon a different cure.

Berzelius had long wanted to visit Paris. The French capital, with its hundred laboratories, was the world center of chemistry. Claude Berthollet, the dean of French chemists, urged him to come.

Sweden and France had been at war, but now, in 1818, that war was ended. The Emperor Napoleon's own marshal, Jean Bernadotte, had been chosen Karl IV Johan, King of Sweden.

With a grant from the king and with the help of the new

Swedish ambassador to France, Berzelius set out on his dream journey.

He was not much interested in splendid buildings and the art galleries of Paris. But he reveled in attending lectures and meeting famous chemists. He was welcomed in the salon of Lavoisier's widow, the proud Comptesse, who had regained her husband's fortune and regularly entertained the most exciting French thinkers. He was shown collections of rare and beautiful minerals. He was invited to work in Berthollet's personal laboratory where he calculated the atomic weight of hydrogen, nitrogen and carbon.

Word arrived from home that he had been appointed Secretary of the Royal Swedish Academy of Science. With that appointment would come at last a comfortable income, a permanent laboratory and an apartment. He was, he decided, one of the luckiest men on earth.

Before his return to the north, he traveled with two younger Swedes by rickety stagecoach and on horseback to see the astonishing "Puys", the mountains of southern France. He was fascinated by the slim black basalt outcroppings with their strange flat tops where two millennia ago the Romans had built temples to their gods and later Christians raised cathedrals.

Ever since his boyhood in the fields and forests of Östergötland, Berzelius had marveled at natural wonders. Now he climbed the steep Puys thrown up by long ago volcanoes and trembled as he wondered whether human beings might have seen those dazzling eruptions.

All in all, the dramatic land of the Puys seemed to Berzelius uniquely beautiful. But in its own way, so was Sweden. He was strong and well again. It was time to go home.

On his return journey, he visited fellow chemists in Switzerland and Germany, indignantly sketching on his way the German students with their straggly mustaches, long hair and baggy jackets. These unkempt students called themselves "romantics," lovers of emotion and poetry. Berzelius was a worshipper of reason.

His place in his native land was now secure. As the powerful and strong-willed Secretary of the Royal Academy, he had become Sweden's scientific authority. He began publication of the Annual Survey of Progress in the Sciences. For decades he could make or break careers by his choice of material for inclusion in the Survey.

His activities were many. He urged teaching science and natural history in Swedish high schools. Traditionalists argued that the preservation of the government, of the monarchy itself, depended on the study of Latin. For his part, Berzelius thought it scandalous that Sweden's clergymen did not understand the barometer or the phases of the moon.

He traveled often and exchanged hundreds of frank and colorful letters with foreign scientists. He continued his own research.

His ever increasing fame brought him exotic samples for chemical analysis— ancient mortar from Egypt, mineral waters and meteorites from around the world, even, from Canada, the gastric juices of a trapper who had suffered a gunshot wound in his stomach!

Berzelius always remained concerned with practical, medical problems. He was an early member of the Swedish Medical Society. He fought hard for medical schools which, like his beloved Caroline Institute, would be attached to hospitals where students could get practical experience. He was enraged by the vendors who sold worthless medicines and the society doctors who "cured" their rich patients with "animal magnetism" which he thought traded on sick people's gullibility. Remembering the drunken housewives of his childhood, he was active in the temperance movement.

In 1834, a cholera epidemic swept through Sweden. In one three-week period, over two thousand people were infected, and half of them died. As a health commissioner, Berzelius organized sanitary work. He was indignant with doctors who declared that sanitary measures were useless since the epidemic was caused by the stars. Berzelius could not guess that fifty years later Robert Koch would isolate the comma-shaped cholera bacillus. He did notice that cholera patients lost a great deal of water which must, in turn, he thought, thicken the blood and bring about death. In recent times, a simple process of compensating for loss of body fluid has indeed decreased the rate of cholera deaths.

Fortunately, the Swedish epidemic soon ended. Berzelius was spared, but he had begun to realize that even a man with his passionate enthusiasm could grow old. Old men could be lonely.

He had thought about marriage several times in the past. Once he had even thought about it seriously, he admitted. But until the age of forty, he had earned hardly enough money to feed and house himself much less a family. Then, too, he had been fiercely dedicated to his work.

Now, urged by his friends, he began to look about him. In 1835 when he was fifty-six years old, he proposed to Johanna Elizabeth Poppius, the daughter of a long-time friend and high government official. Betty Poppius was a tiny woman with delicate features and a proud carriage. She was only twenty-four years old but she had known her famous suitor all her life. She had danced with him around the Swedish Jul tree for twenty Christmases. Both she and her family readily accepted his proposal.

The couple celebrated an elaborate and happy wedding day. King Karl IV Johan declared the bridegroom a baron and granted him a splendid coat of arms. He was now entitled to attend the Rikstag, or Parliament's House of Nobility, though he did not go often. He had no interest in politics and thought that the sensible men in the House of Nobility were those who said nothing.

Soon after his wedding, Berzelius announced that his Betty had far more intelligence than most women. A wife who is one's good friend is the greatest blessing a man can have, he decided. He was not rid of money problems since he had never lost the habit of lending money to friends and relatives, but his wife handled their limited finances well.

By now Berzelius had received twelve Royal Orders and was a member of nearly a hundred scientific societies. He was a possessor of so many metals that wearing them all would have made him look ridiculous, he said.

During his last years, he continued to assemble the Annual Survey of Progress in the Sciences and to revise the giant general chemistry textbook, begun forty years ago. He could still say that "an unfulfilled task burns within me until it is completed." Even now he could not abandon his skill at analysis and turned to ever more exotic substances. He studied an embalming fluid sold by a man whom he suspected of cheating people. And he analyzed the bile of an Amazon tiger python brought by a wanderer to Stockholm.

To his deep distress, Berzelius' "dualistic" electrochemical theory of compounds was being torn apart by younger chemists. It was not opposing electrical charges but the arrangement of elements within a compound which held those compounds together, the younger chemists claimed. No one could yet know that the late nineteenth century discovery of the electron would make possible a truer understanding of the bonds which hold atoms together.

A theory can be a bridge to the truth but, as Berzelius himself warned, it can sometimes lead to error and mistake.

Even a genius may take a wrong bridge when the guideposts are not yet clear.

In 1847, scientists of many countries gathered in Copenhagen to honor Berzelius. A year later he died in Stockholm.

His statue, commissioned by the Swedish Royal Society and unveiled in 1858, still stands in Verzelii Park. It presents a masterful figure in flowing bronze robe looking confidently out toward the great northern city where he was for so long king of science and lover of "truth, the angel of light."

Chapter V

Justus von Liebig
Master Teacher

Paint dealer George Liebig of Darmstadt had eight children. Of this large brood Justus, the fiery second son, born in 1803, was his father's most eager helper. The boy haunted the family shop, learning to mix not only lacquers and paints but drugs, dyes and boot polish. Even when the treacherous brews foamed up about his arms and face, he did not stop his work.

For Justus loved the excitement of finding out how substances reacted with each other. Especially he loved explosives.

When a wandering peddler came to town with fireworks and toy torpedoes, the people of Darmstadt hailed him as a magician. But Justus did not believe in magic. He wheedled the peddler's secret from him. The propellent which sent toy torpedoes bursting across the market square was in fact a chemical called silver fulminate.

The boy hurried back to his father's shop and soon began experimenting with silver fulminate.

But he was not content. He wanted to know more than he could ever learn from his own crude results or from his studies at the local high school. That school was a dull place, he thought.

Fortunately Ludwig X, ruler of the tiny duchy of Hesse-Darmstadt, was an enlightened man. He was not only rebuilding his small capital city, hardly changed since medieval times. He also opened his private library to the town people.

Justus delved into the treasures he found there, reading the books from side to side and top to bottom of the ample shelves. Eventually he had read the thirty-two volumes of the dictionary of chemistry, as well as other science texts.

When he was not reading, helping his father in the paint shop or dreaming through his high school classes, he visited the small manufactories of Darmstadt. He went to the soap makers. He went to the tanners and dyers. He went to the blacksmiths and the brass makers. Everywhere he learned the formulae for these trades, developing a prodigious memory including what he himself called "eye-memory." In later years he could identify a wide range of chemicals by sight alone.

None of this activity won him good grades in the class room. At examination time the school principal scolded him angrily. He was a plague to his teachers and a sorrow to his parents! What, the principal asked, did he mean to do with himself?

Justus replied that he was going to become a chemist. The other boys roared with laughter. Nobody in Germany earned a living as a chemist!

Many men did support themselves as pharmacists. After all, people were forever getting sick, forever wanting cures.

The next step seemed clear. At fifteen Justus left school. He set out for the nearby village of Appenheim to be apprenticed to a pharmacist.

The arrangement did not last long. The boy with dreams of pure chemistry dancing in his head hated sweeping out the pharmacy shop, cleaning shelves, washing bottles. He said later that his stern master dismissed him because of the explosions which blew out the windows of the apprentice's attic room.

Justus came home. But Darmstadt could no longer hold him. There was another road to follow.

George Liebig supplied chemicals to Karl Wilhelm Kastner, professor of chemistry at the newly established University of Bonn, to whom he introduced his seventeen-year-old son. Kastner recognized at once the talent of the slim, energetic boy with the intense dark eyes. Justus had never finished high school, a requirement for entering the University, but Kastner ignored the rules. He admitted the boy to his classes.

Still Justus was not satisfied. No science laboratories were open to students at the University. Lectures and books furnished the only instruction. What was more, Professor Kastner, despite his kindness, turned out to know very little about chemical analysis. He was quite unable to determine the various elements of which minerals were composed.

Disappointed though he was, Justus followed when Kastner received a new appointment at the University of Erlangen. At Erlangen Justus worked hard. He wrote in a very short time a slim book called *A Comparative Study of the Systems of Chemistry*, He organized a student club to read and discuss the latest findings in physics and chemistry. He set about mastering the languages which he had scorned in high school. He also joined in lively political debates and protests. Students at Erlangen, as at other German universities, frequently fought with the police. Justus was not one to stay away from excitement. Suddenly, for his battling, he found himself sentenced to a term in prison.

Once again Professor Kastner came to the rescue. He sent to the Duke of Hesse-Darmstadt a copy of Justus' book, *A Comparative Study*, together with a letter of glowing praise for the endangered young author. The Duke replied with a pardon. He also promised money.

Now at last Justus could leave what was then the limited

world of German science. "Chemistry is a French science. It was created by Lavoisier of immortal memory," said a Frenchman.

Justus would go to Paris.

He arrived in the great city, a nineteen-year-old German with a brand new, slightly dubious Ph.D. He had not completed his doctoral thesis. He never would. But loyal Professor Kastner had granted the degree. Kastner must have been eager to get his stormy petrel away from student street fights and the clutches of the Erlangen police.

In Paris Justus was first admitted to the private laboratory of Gaultier de Claubry, a professor of chemistry in the school of pharmacy. De Claubry was worthy but not the most notable Parisian chemist. No matter. Glad of his chance, Justus began research on the fulminates, those highly explosive substances which reminded him of the peddler and his toy torpedoes.

At the end of a year he was invited to speak before the French Academy of Science.

Among those who gathered round to congratulate him was a somewhat old-fashioned looking gentleman who invited him to dinner on the following Sunday. Justus happily accepted but in his excitement forgot to ask for his host's name and address.

Later he learned that he had missed dinner with none other than the Ambassador from Prussia to the court of the King of France — the famous explorer and geographer, Alexander von Humboldt.

Justus rushed to the Ambassador's home to apologize for his rudeness. Von Humboldt promptly invited him to dinner for the next Sunday. There the twenty-year-old found himself sitting at table with the noted organic chemist, Joseph Louis Gay-Lussac.

Gay-Lussac had begun his own career by making a solo

ascent in a hot air balloon to 23,000 feet in order to study the earth's atmosphere at different levels. Since then, among other accomplishments, he had collaborated with von Humboldt on a paper which hinted at what would later be called the law of the combination of gases by volume. He had worked on those methods of chemical analysis of which Professor Kastner was so ignorant. He had studied the chemistry of plants and animals, was a professor at the Sorbonne and a member of the French administration of explosives and saltpetres. He was much interested in the treacherous fulminic acids. The very man, as von Humboldt had guessed, to invite young Justus von Liebig into his laboratory!

In that laboratory during the year 1823-24 Justus learned much about chemical analysis. He developed skill at blowing glass and making equipment. All the while he continued his research.

One startling day he read an article by another young German, Friedrich Wöhler, then studying with Berzelius in Sweden. Wohler announced the formula for what he called cyanic acid. It was the same substance that Justus had labeled fulminic acid.

This Wöhler is wrong! Justus declared. But he repeated Wöhler's experiments only to get the same result. The truth was that the cyanic and fulminic acids, so different in appearance, were made up of exactly the same elements in exactly the same proportions.

There was only one explanation.

The atoms must be arranged differently in the two substances! This was the discovery of what Wöhler's great Swedish teacher would call "isomers."

Wöhler wrote to suggest that he and Justus collaborate. They met and became friends. Wöhler was gentle, calm and careful, never liking a fight, always ready to laugh at life.

Justus was intense and fiery, not caring whom he offended, even liking to offend his opponents when he thought he was right. Together they would publish fifteen important papers.

On one matter the two agreed at once. Fulminic acid had brought them together. Regretfully now they must leave it alone.

It was far too dangerous. One recent experiment had exploded in Justus' face, leaving him deaf and nearly blind for days.

But now in 1824 it was time for him to return to Germany. His friend Alexander von Humboldt had decided that he would make an excellent teacher. Humboldt wrote to the Duke in Darmstadt, urging him to find an appointment for the young man.

The Duke responded with the offer of a position at the small University of Giessen. No one could have guessed that the quiet, tree-shaded institution, founded in 1607, with no scientific reputation whatever, would come to be called the Justus Liebig University. Nor could anyone, including von Humboldt, have guessed that a great century in German chemistry was beginning. The once sleepy little University of Giessen would play a vital role.

Herr Professor Liebig wasted no time in dreams about the future. He meant to make the future happen. No chemistry lab was open to students at Giessen. There would be one!

Buffeted by Liebig's demands, the University obtained space in an abandoned police barracks. Upstairs was an apartment to which the professor brought his bride Henrietta, a brave young woman, undaunted by her new husband's career or by his fiery temper. One small room doubled as her laundry and, when she was not using it, a laboratory.

What mysterious fumes must have hung over Henrietta's soaking clothes! Fortunately her husband, along with his other talents, knew how to make excellent soap.

Liebig's main laboratory area had space for twelve students, their work benches, chemicals and equipment. The equipment the young professor himself bought by taking out a personal loan. Students needed test tubes (which had recently replaced wine glasses in general laboratory use), retorts and a coal stove for heating these glass vessels. They also needed blowpipes for producing flames and delicate balances for weighing.

There was no ventilation for the crowded, unheated room with its ever present film of coal dust. When glass vessels cracked and dangerous acids escaped, professor and students threw open the windows and rushed out-of-doors, into sunshine, rain or snow.

Simple though it was, Liebig was founding what was to become the greatest laboratory for the teaching of chemistry anyone had ever known, the model for chemistry laboratories to this day.

Soon students from near and far began to flock to Giessen.

Alexander von Humboldt had been right. Liebig was a remarkable teacher. He was not an orator, but his voice was musical and exciting. In his lectures students saw, as one of them said, "the tree of chemistry," not simply "a sackful of dried leaves."

In his enthusiasm Liebig often flubbed demonstrations. Solutions turned yellow not red, red not yellow, or behaved in other unexpected ways. The lecture went on, as clear and well organized as though following some carefully written outline.

The outline was in Liebig's head. He had before him only three or four scribbled notes.

With his by now prodigious knowledge he could walk around a laboratory in which each student was working on a different experiment, advise and predict the results. All the while he could notice when a single test tube was out of place.

In the early years of the nineteenth century organic chemistry, the study of substances which contain carbon, was, so Friedrich Wöhler said, like a dark forest with few paths. To break a way through the tangled woodland required endless work and imagination.

Older methods of analysis had been time-consuming and often inaccurate. Liebig dazzled his students by his ingenious new methods. Among other pieces of equipment he used the "Kaiapparat," a triumph of the glass blower's skill. It was a clever triangular array of glass bottles by which the different elements which made up a chemical compound could be determined.

Liebig did not win his great popularity as a teacher by pampering the young men who came to study with him. (Young women were not admitted to German universities.) He stubbornly refused to teach simple formulae for dye-making or drug-mixing but insisted on a knowledge of basic chemistry.

Sometimes he gave a series of difficult examinations to frighten away all but the most talented and determined students. Once accepted, each young man must learn glass blowing, make his own equipment and master a difficult organic chemistry textbook. After the first bewildering weeks he was introduced to "the shelf of a hundred bottles." The challenge was to identify the hundred substances by chemical analysis.

One American student left a record of his daily schedule. He, like his fellow students, got out of bed every morning at 5:30 and ate a breakfast of milk and biscuit. At 6:10 he attended a lecture demonstration, at 7:00 another lecture. By 8:15 he was in the laboratory working on his own research.

At 11:05 he broke off that work to attend one of Liebig's lectures. At noon he lunched and by one o'clock was back at his research where he worked til 6:30. Some evenings he took a swim in the nearby river before returning to his room for more milk and biscuit at 8 o'clock. Two hours of reading chemical magazines and thinking about chemical problems lasted until 10:30 when he blew out his candle and slid into bed.

Small wonder that the young men who survived this schedule became noted scientists in their own right!

Over time, Liebig's salary was doubled, tripled and by 1840 was ten times the meager 300 florins he had first been paid. He was given more assistants, more laboratory space.

In 1839 the University financed for him a handsome chemistry building with a fine pillared portico and excellent equipment. They dared not let their treasure slip away to the beckoning cities of Antwerp, St. Petersburg and Vienna.

In 1845 the paint dealer's son became Justus von Liebig, a nobleman, a baron!

His life was full. Not only was he the head of a fine laboratory. He and Henrietta had five children, among them the adventurous George named after Justus' father. He had a home with a garden where students and faculty members assembled regularly. At these gatherings von Liebig talked freely about chemistry and played games with his children and friends. He played games to win, demanding that everyone about him be silent while he thought out his strategy.

His interests had become very broad. He had begun writing his "Familiar Letters on Chemistry," widely published in German newspapers. He had become co-editor of "Annalen," a pharmaceutical magazine which in a very few years was also publishing outstanding articles on chemistry. He, as editor, responded to many of these papers.

His responses were often biting criticisms which brought fiery answers from angry authors.

Von Liebig said that he criticized so often because he spent his days with young men who would think he agreed with error if he kept silent.

Only his friend Wöhler could safely scold him for his attacks on their colleagues.

"To make war is of no use," Wöhler wrote. "You merely consume yourself and ruin your liver and your nerves... Imagine yourself in 1900 when we both have decomposed again into carbonic acid, water and ammonia... Who would then care whether we lived at peace or at strife? No one. But your good ideas, the new facts you have discovered, these purged of all that is inessential, will be known and recognized to the remotest time. But how do I come to counsel the lion to eat sugar?"

The lion did not eat sugar! Writing about another of his victims, von Liebig declared, "Poggendorff is a fool... All the bile which had long been concentrating in me on his account, I have now poured out upon his head, and I feel relieved to know that the miserable half relationship has become clear upon enmity. I am bound to defend my convictions to the very death."

Luckily death was far away, and von Liebig never poured his bile out upon his dear friend Wöhler.

Together they continued work in "pure" science which not only solved old mysteries but led to such practical results as the improvement of mirrors and photography.

Von Liebig was pleased and proud when Wöhler by heating aluminum cyanate prepared urea, an organic substance up to that time derived only from animal urine.

The formula for the aluminum cyanate molecule is NH_4OCN, for urea NH_2CONH_2. Both are made up of exactly the same elements — nitrogen, hydrogen, oxygen and carbon — in exactly the same proportions, but the atoms are joined in different patterns. The two compounds are isomers.

Many organic isomers are known today. The four simple elements which make up urea and aluminum cyanate can combine to make millions of different compounds for myriads of different uses.

But Wöhler and von Liebig had already discovered an isomer. This time the truly startling fact was that Wöhler had made an organic substance, urea, from an inorganic or mineral substance.

Many nineteenth century scientists believed that organic compounds, urea among them, would never yield all their secrets, much less be produced in a laboratory. They believed that in addition to chemical elements, plants and animals contained a "vital force" which could not be isolated or measured.

The tactful Wöhler did not directly point out that his artificially produced urea destroyed the notion of a "vital force." Von Liebig spoke for him by announcing that "a new era in science has begun."

His friend had sent a brilliant beam of light into the dark organic forest!

The most important work which the two chemists undertook together led to another discovery. By experimenting with oil of bitter almonds they proved the existence of radicals. Radicals are tightly bound groups of atoms which remain unchanged no matter what is done to them. Although they seldom exist on their own, they appear as essential parts of many organic compounds.

Oil of almonds, for instance, is a liquid whose molecule is made up of the radical C_6H_3CO — seven atoms of carbon, three atoms of hydrogen and one of oxygen — plus one more atom of hydrogen. The molecule of Benzoic acid, a white powder, is made up of exactly the same radical, C_6H_3CO — plus one more atom of hydrogen and one more of oxygen.

In 1838 the friends discovered sixteen new compounds whose make-up could be explained by radical theory. After 1838 their scientific work followed different paths.

Von Liebig liked the excitement of pushing into dark forests. Once a basic discovery had been made he was not interested in working out the details. He turned now to a science which as yet barely existed — agricultural chemistry.

"There is no profession which can be compared in importance to agriculture," he declared. But neither he nor anybody else knew very much about plant or animal nutrition.

For generations farmers had noticed that certain practices increased the yield of their crops. Ground bones scattered over the ground and manure from their animals helped. Rotating crops, letting fields stand idle, even, in hilly country, contour farming helped, too.

Scientists for their part guessed that carbon dioxide, which animals breathe out and plants absorb from the air, was somehow inside the plant split apart by sunlight. The released oxygen was returned to the air, to be breathed in by the animals. The carbon left behind built new plant tissue. Beyond that the nutritional process was a mystery.

Von Liebig with his students set about analyzing the ashes of hundreds of plants. He proved that plants were indeed fed water and carbon dioxide and nitrogen from the air. They took lime, phosphates and potassium from the soil.

When soil did not contain those chemicals, plants did not thrive. Poor crops resulted not only from poor soil but from once rich soil used so often that the nutrients had been sucked out of it. What to do?

Add to the soil the elements it lacked, said von Liebig.

Farmers had never before used chemical fertilizers, but gradually they began to do so. The great fertilizer industries of England and of Germany were born.

But there was a new problem.

Farmers began pouring huge quantities of fertilizer onto their fields and often got no better crops than before. Not surprising, said von Liebig. Each crop required its own appropriate fertilizer. Feeding a crop double the amount of necessary potassium, for instance, but skimping on the necessary phosphate would not increase yield.

Fertilizer was like a chain. A chain with one weak link would break even when the sturdy links were further strengthened. Flawless playing by the violins would not keep a badly played French horn from destroying the beauty of a concert.

With his driving energy von Liebig often made mistakes. One special disappointment was the field he purchased near the University. There he planted several kinds of seed, fertilized the soil and confidently waited for his crops to flourish. Year after year they failed him. At last he recognized that the chemicals he had used to keep the fertilizer from washing away had also kept the plant roots from absorbing the minerals.

Von Liebig was, after all, town bred, not farm bred. A practical farmer would not have made some of his mistakes, but mistakes never stopped him. He admitted them and worked on. All the while he was publishing a stream of books and papers which were influencing farmers around the world. Even his mistakes were often useful since they inspired other scientists to make further experiments and correct the master's errors. Nutrition of animals and humans presented even deeper mysteries.

The famous alchemist Paracelsus in the sixteenth century

had said that an Alchemist lived in every man's stomach. This Alchemist digested the food a man — or an animal — ate, cleverly separating the good food from the bad. The Alchemist inside an ostrich knew how to digest iron. A salamander could make a meal on fire.

Probably even Paracelsus didn't believe in a captive midget in a peaked hat busily sorting out people's dinners, but he had neither the words nor the knowledge to give a clearer account.

Von Liebig, living three centuries later, was better equipped. He had always been fiercely opposed to the idea of magic. He set out to explain digestion and nutrition scientifically. His theories would lead in time to the discovery of enzymes, those large groups of proteins essential to the process upon which life depends.

With all his theories von Liebig never scorned practical work and commonplace materials.

He experimented with sauerkraut. He wanted to improve rye bread, broth for sick people, food for infants. With an American student he developed a baking powder which German cooks used for many years. Concerned that poor people couldn't afford meat, he created a beef extract which, he thought, relieved exhaustion and "mental weakness." The beef extract, quality controlled, was widely sold with von Liebig's picture on the package.

One day von Liebig was faced with a quite different puzzle. He was called from his laboratory to testify at a murder trial. The body of a Countess had been found in her apartment dead and partially burned. Her house boy was accused of killing her. The defense argued that the Countess had been a heavy drinker. Because of the high level of alcohol in her body she had burst into flames: a case of spontaneous combustion. This defense had been successful in numerous nineteenth century trials.

Von Liebig pointed out that the human body is at least seventy-five per cent water. No matter how heavily the Countess had been drinking, her body could not have risen above the boiling point of water and burst into flames.

A young architecture student, a spectator at the trial, was inspired by von Liebig's testimony. Friedrich August Kekule abandoned architecture to become probably the most important chemist ever trained at Giessen.

In 1858 even Justus von Liebig began to lose momentum. He accepted a less taxing professorship at the University of Munich. Over his years at Giessen he had trained seven hundred young pharmacists and chemists. Now he decided not to take any more research students. He turned toward lecturing and increased writing. In that writing his old combative spirit lived on. His last published work included replies to his many critics.

If those critics abounded, so, too, did the generations of his students who carried his ideas to laboratories around the world. "He *is* chemistry," one of those students wrote.

As for the dearest friendship of von Liebig's life, that never wavered.

Before his death in 1873 he wrote to Wöhler, "We will not be able to greet each other for long, but when we have become dust, the bonds which held us together in life will still link us in the minds of living man as a unique example of two men who worked together harmoniously, ever true friends, without jealousy or envy."

Theirs was the greatest comradeship known to the history of chemistry. Von Liebig himself has been called the greatest teacher. His laboratory, preserved in Giessen, is a memorial to the energetic and creative scientist of whom it has been said, "He felt in himself a call for an accomplishment for which no man's strength and lifetime would be sufficient."

Chapter VI

Dmitri Mendeleyev
Creator of the Periodic Table

Dmitri Ivanovich Mendeleyev was born on a frozen winter's day in 1834 in Tobolsk, capital of old Siberia. He was the youngest and fourteenth of the Mendeleyev children. Or was he the sixteenth? Or the seventeenth? Storytellers disagree.

Nobody disagrees about the bravery of the mother or the brilliance of the son.

Maria Dmitrievna Korniliev was descended on one side of her family from the Tatars, that terrifying Golden Horde which had once swept across Asia, across Russia and into the heart of Europe. By the nineteenth century, the Tatar fortresses in western Siberia had long since crumbled. But Maria's family was important in Tobolsk. They had set up the first printing press in Siberia, founded a newspaper and, not many miles outside the city, built a glass factory.

Maria herself married Ivan Pavlovich Mendeleyev, a scholar and principal of the local high school. Their youngest son Mitia was, from the beginning, a clever student, excited by science and mathematics, gagging on Latin. Outside of school, the boy was tutored by a learned brother-in-law, an exile to Siberia who had plotted against Czar Nicholas I.

Over the years Tobolsk had become a city of exiles. Not all had been banished there. Some had come voluntarily, dreaming of religious and political freedom in a sparsely settled land. Countless others, condemned people, innocents and criminals alike, had trudged, chained and hungry, through Tobolsk on their way to their government's loathsome prisons in eastern Siberia.

Though her roots were in Tobolsk, Maria wanted a wider world for her talented son. Widowed, with the family glass factory destroyed by fire, she turned westward. Not towards St. Petersburg where her husband had been a student. To Moscow. There, so she planned, her Mitia could attend the greatest of all Russian institutions of learning, the University of Moscow.

The goal lay more than a thousand miles distant, far beyond the forbidding Ural mountains. Maria was undeterred. She purchased a telega, a springless horse-drawn wagon, large enough for herself, Mitia, her frail youngest daughter Elizabeth and their few possessions.

As they set out, the three must have looked wistfully back at Tobolsk. The city climbed the sloping banks of the Irtysh River up to the turreted walls of the Kremlin with its guard houses, lacy stone monasteries, churches and cathedral. But Maria must also have seen in her mind's eye a greater Kremlin on which the fortress of Tobolsk had been modeled.

After a hard journey, she and her children reached Moscow. She did not reach her dream. The University of Moscow, whose founder, the great Lomonosov, had lied about his peasant birth in order to gain an education, refused to enroll a Siberian. Truth to tell, the registrars probably saw little promise in the blond, gangling sixteen-year-old with his odd accent, unfashionable clothing and diploma from a far away, unknown high school.

The three Mendeleyevs set out on a further journey. This time they travelled hopefully north to St. Petersburg. But the University of St. Petersburg also turned Mitia away. Day after day Maria knocked on official doors until, at last, she found a kindly listener who had known her husband in their student days.

With the help of this friend, Mitia was admitted to the city's chief teacher training school. This was far from the glorious appointment of which Maria had dreamed but it was a beginning. Mitia could study and his expenses would be paid, even if meagerly. Later, perhaps.... perhaps....

Maria would never know what lay beyond that "perhaps." Both she and her daughter died not long after the little family was settled.

A stranger to the splendid city, poor and alone but in love with science, Mendeleyev immersed himself in his studies. Before long his instructors thought that he, too, was fatally ill. He was sent south to the Crimea and to the city of Odessa to teach and await death.

He did not die. Hiking in the warm, soft air amid wheat fields, orchards and vineyards never seen in his gray Siberian homeland, he grew strong. He returned to St. Petersburg and in 1856 received the degree Master of Chemistry from the teacher training institute. He was appointed a *privatdozent*. This was an unsalaried teaching position but Mendeleyev was used to life with an empty purse. He survived with the help of small fees from his students.

When he was twenty-six, he went on a government fellowship to Germany's famous old University of Heidelberg. Despite some talented scholars, Russian science was poorly financed and undeveloped. In Heidelberg, Mendeleyev would have a chance to do more original research and meet new ideas. He set up a chemical laboratory in his small apartment. In 1860 he took an active part in the Karlsruhe Chemical Congress, the first international scientific meeting.

There speakers pointed out the basic distinction between atoms and molecules and the importance of atomic weights.

A half-century after Dalton's notable papers, it was now universally agreed that an atom is the smallest portion of an element that can take part in a chemical reaction. Atomic weight is the average of the masses of all naturally occurring isotopes of an element. Isotopes of an element are chemically identical but have differing numbers of particles in the atomic nucleus.

A molecule is a cluster of two or more atoms. It is the smallest portion of a chemical compound which can exist independently and keep the properties of the original substance.

Mendeleyev went back to St. Petersburg in 1861, his head awhirl. It was not facts alone which the new chemistry had given him. Sixty-three chemical elements had now been discovered, nearly double the number known to Lavoisier. But there were great questions. How to see a pattern in the bewildering array? Surely the universe and chemistry with it were no random hodge-podge but an ordered system.

Even Mendeleyev could not solve such a puzzle overnight.

In 1861 he published a textbook on Organic Chemistry. The book was widely used and won the first of many prizes awarded its author. In 1863 he accepted the Chair of Technology at the University of St. Petersburg which not many years before had denied him admission. In that same year he became interested in the development of the new Russian petroleum industry at Baku on the Caspian Sea. In 1863, also, he married a Siberian woman, Feozva Nikitichna Lescheva.

By now Mendeleyev was tall and shaggy and wore a flowing beard like the Muzhiks, the peasant men of old Siberia. He had a deep devotion to children and his students but he was quick-tempered, quick-moving and inward, not at all concerned with being like other people. He was clever with his hands and for relaxation became expert in bookbinding and suitcase making.

He was also an eager traveller and had dreams of adventure. He reveled in the swashbuckling novels of the French romantic author Alexandre Dumas, in Jules Verne's exciting *Around the World in 80 Days* and the American Indian stories of James Fenimore Cooper with their exotic heroes.

In 1868 when Mendeleyev was only thirty-four, he helped to found the Russian Chemical Society and published his second major book *Principles of Chemistry*. "Truly his monument," this book has been called. It has appeared in many editions and translations. Copies stand on the shelves of American university libraries today. The author's voice still speaks eloquently from the yellowed pages.

"Knowing how contented, free and joyous is life in the realm of science, one fervently wishes that many would enter its portals," he says. "The time has arrived when a knowledge of physics and chemistry forms as important a part of education as that of the classics two centuries ago."

"Science is a universal heritage," the persuasive voice goes on, "and it is only just to give the highest honor in science.... to those who are first able to convince others of its authenticity."

As for himself, as author of the *Principles,* "his continual endeavor has been to bring the scattered facts of chemistry within the domain of law." "The edifice of science not only required material but also a plan."

Mendeleyev was, of course, not alone in wanting to find such a grand plan. Good chemists before him had taken part in the search. Some had thought that chemical elements were related in triads, or groups of three. One observer, who was much mocked, saw the elements arranged in octaves like the octaves in music.

Before Mendeleyev could propose his own configuration, he not only continued new research but repeated many experiments which had been performed by others. The essence of science is, after all, that experimental results must be reproducible at any time and place. If they cannot be reproduced, the results are not to be trusted. Mendeleyev found that he could not trust all of the data in the scientific literature, and he boldly made corrections for nine elements.

Still, where was the pattern?

Luckily, chemistry had by now the practical system of notation proposed by Jöns Jakob Berzelius. Hydrogen, the lightest element known in the universe and the most plentiful, was H. Oxygen was O, phosphorous P. Of the symbols requiring two letters, silver was Ag, based on the old Latin name for the metal. Gold was Au. All in all, Mendeleyev found the system remarkably easy to use, much superior to the complicated arrangements of white and black circles which John Dalton had once suggested and stubbornly defended.

But notation alone will not solve mysteries. Exactly how in the end Mendeleyev evolved what he called the Periodic Table is the stuff of fantasy. Some storytellers have insisted that he claimed to have seen the entire Periodic Table in a dream. His own notes which are preserved, marked with a breakfast cup stain, seem to prove that he did not dream but did, in fact, come to his revolutionary conclusion on a single winter's day in 1869.

He had apparently meant to visit local cheese factories that morning. For some reason he abandoned those plans. Instead he stayed at home and set about making a systematic list of the sixty-three chemical elements, arranged according to their atomic weights. After two or three unsatisfactory and depressing attempts, he wrote out, on small white cards, the symbols for all the elements along with their atomic weights and physical and chemical properties. He pinned these cards on his study walls.

One can imagine him, long-legged, long-bearded, pacing about the room studying the cards, jostling them from place to place in a kind of chemical solitaire. So at last he saw the order he sought and created his Periodic Table. The table arranged the elements according to their successive atomic weights with hydrogen, the lightest element, in the lead. Today's charts are based on atomic number, that is, the number of electrons in the nucleus of an atom, but the basic arrangement is unchanged.

The Periodic Table was set up in coherent columns, separating metals, metalloids and non-metals, each having its own properties. Among the important chemical properties, for example, is reactivity. Some substances, like hydrogen, react with other substances so readily that they are rarely found "free" or uncombined in nature. Other substances, like iron or silver or gold, react less readily. A few, like the "noble" gases helium and neon, react scarcely at all. All this would be represented by position on the chart.

At first glance, the Periodic Table almost appears like a mysterious kind of crossword puzzle. A crossword puzzle has blanks. Mendeleyev, too, found empty spaces, unoccupied by any known chemicals. But nature leaves no gaps. A Periodic Table is true or it is not true, he thought. Confident of his own inspiration, he predicted that the gaps in his Periodic Table would, in time, be filled by newly discovered elements. He boldly gave them names, atomic weights and physical and chemical properties.

As an example, he said the as yet undiscovered "eka boron" would look like a metal, would not be dissolved in either water or ammonia, would be dissolved in acids and would weigh one gram per cubic centimeter. These prophesies were published in "The Journal of the Russian Chemical Society" in 1871.

Only four years later a French chemist found "eka aluminum", now called gallium, in a zinc blend from the Pyrenees Mountains. Another four years later, "eka boron" or scandium, was identified. In the next decade, a German discovered "eka silicon" or germanium. "There is no doubt that this is Mendeleyev's 'eka silicon'," the German wrote. "The correspondence is remarkable, even amazing."

The theory for which much of his research since his student days had prepared Mendeleyev was confirmed. Chemists need no longer seek a pattern for the elements. World-wide, they accepted the Periodic Law. It is unchallenged today.

In the year 1876 there was drama in Mendeleyev's private life. His first marriage had brought him two children but little happiness. For much of the year, husband and wife lived apart. Then, in 1876, Mendeleyev met and fell deeply in love with a seventeen-year-old art student, Anna Ivanovna Popov. His wife was, in time, persuaded to grant him a divorce, and he promptly and joyously married Anna with whom he would have four children.

The Russian Orthodox Church allowed divorce but forbade remarriage for seven years. Noblemen complained to the Czar that his favorite scientist was a bigamist.

Unperturbed, the Czar replied, "Mendeleyev may have two wives but I have only one Mendeleyev."

There were still other dramas in that year, 1876. The Minister of Finance and the Russian Technical Society directed Mendeleyev to visit the United States.

In far away western Pennsylvania, chemists had observed oil seeping out of the ground. On August 27, 1859, while Mendeleyev had been a student, the first oil well in history had been drilled near the small town of Titusville, Pennsylvania.

Now there was a booming "oil rush" in the area. Fortunes were being made in towns like Tionesta and Tidioute along the Allegheny River.

The Indian names may have reminded Mendeleyev of his favorite Cooper novels. More importantly, knowledge gained from observing this successful new industry might help Russia develop its own lagging Baku oil fields.

In June, Mendeleyev, with a student interpreter, set sail from France on the S.S. Labrador. The eleven-day passage was gray and foggy. The city of New York, where the Labrador docked, turned out to be a town of narrow cobblestone streets which did not impress a man from Peter the Great's beautiful city.

Mendeleyev knew little about American history. He seems to have come eagerly to the new world, thinking he would find a fairy tale society where tyranny and injustice did not exist and where fundamental science was honored.

He had, instead, come to a still young country, struggling with the racial prejudice, bitterness and corruption which followed the Civil War. American glory days in science lay in the future. For now, chemists were largely concerned with immediate, practical results. Mendeleyev put his Differential Barometer on display at the Centennial Exposition in Philadelphia. But Americans did not know who he was and he seems to have met few chemists. In Pittsburgh, on the Fourth of July, exploding firecrackers kept him awake far into the night!

He found greater satisfaction in the oil fields of northwestern Pennsylvania. He spent several weeks inspecting the tall, thumping derricks which forested the hillsides and the pipelines which carried away the rich oil. There he admired the skill and energy of the scientists and engineers. They had much to teach him.

The foaming thunder of Niagara Falls impressed him, too. But the heat of a New York summer made a Siberian ill. He returned early to Russia. As he customarily did after any important experience, he published a lengthy report. Based on what he had seen, he made recommendations for improving the output of the Baku oil fields, including the lifting of heavy government restrictions.

Over the years Mendeleyev continued his interests both in how oil had originally been formed beneath the surface of the earth and in how it might be extracted and used for human good. He could not guess that the most productive "oil gusher" in history would be drilled one day in his native Siberia, east of Tobolsk.

Mendeleyev had a mind and energy which, octopus-like, reached out into numerous aspects of Russian industry and life. He did both theoretical and practical work on gases and fluids, on meteorology and agricultural chemistry, on coal, salt, metals, even gunpowder, though he was always a man of peace.

His interests even sent him on a Jules Verne adventure of his own. He had long investigated gases. Steam is a gas. Air is a gas. Helium, lighter than air, is the gas which, when pumped into a party balloon, shapes it and makes it rise.

In 1783, the Montgolfier brothers of France had launched a hot air balloon over Paris, with the first flying crew known to history — a sheep, a rooster and a duck! In the century that had passed, much experimenting had been done with balloons, and Mendeleyev was keenly interested in them.

In 1887 he decided to go aloft to study a total eclipse of the sun. Just before the ascent he realized that the waiting balloon could carry only one man. Precipitously, he dismissed the pilot. Though he had never before been at the controls of a balloon, he maneuvered his craft into the darkening sky. Later, deftly arranging guide rope and ballast, he descended safely back to earth.

Despite Mendeleyev's adventurous spirit, his brilliance and his devotion to Russia, his relationship with his university had become uneasy. Ever since Czar Peter the Great had imported German scientists to bring the learning of western Europe to his vast and undeveloped empire, Russian and German scientists had competed with each other for high position. The great Lomonosov, founder of the University of Moscow, had lost a coveted appointment to a German. Now, Mendeleyev was denied the chair in chemical technology at the Imperial Academy of Science. His successful opponent was a German.

It was a time of wide-spread unrest in Russia. Many people were rebelling against the tyranny of the Czar. Patriot though he was, Mendeleyev objected to the harsh treatment which the University of St. Petersburg meted out to protesting students.

In 1890, he himself protested by resigning his professorship. For three years he was without a position. Then, in 1893, he became Chief of the Russian Chamber of Weights and Measures.

A trivial job for a man who had contributed so much to his country? No, not in Mendeleyev's hands. Systems of weights and measures reach back thousands of years to the ancient Babylonians and Egyptians who left their records on temples and pyramids. They reach back many centuries before King Henry I of England decreed, so legend reports, that the length of a yard should be the distance from the tip of the Royal nose to the tip of his outstretched thumb. All organized society needs uniform and accurate methods of measurement.

Under Mendeleyev, the Chamber of Weights and

Measures became a much needed institution of pure research.

One challenge was the creation of metal alloys and the manufacture of prototypes both for traditional Russian units of measurement and for metric units. With the growth of international trade, there was a pressing need for standardization. A measure of length must be precisely the same in Siberia and in Timbuktu. Weight would, of course, vary slightly because of the pull of gravitation. A man on the top of Mt. Everest weighs less than the same man in the same suit in Death Valley.

The metric system, based on multiples of ten, had been devised by the French Academy in 1791. The earliest definition of a meter was one ten-millionth of the distance from the Equator to the North Pole — not too easy to check at first hand! Metallic prototypes were needed and of a material which would not be changed by heat, cold, moisture or the oxygen in the air itself. Mendeleyev's and other national laboratories attacked the problem.

An alloy composed of platinum and iridium would in time be found to be most useful for measuring both length and weight. By 1960, the wave-length of light, not an arc of the Earth's circumference, would provide the standard on which prototypes would be based, but those developments were far in the future.

Of more immediate use, Mendeleyev's Chamber set up a new system for inspecting industrial products so that consumers would not be cheated by dishonest manufacturers. He founded "The Russian Journal of Metrology" devoted to this newly-recognized science of weights and measures.

Mendeleyev was no longer a young man. He was rich in honors. Over the years he had received more than a hundred medals, honorary doctorates, and other awards. He had written hundreds of books and papers. His last book, completed during the final months of his life, *Toward an Understanding of Russia,* predicted an expanding future for his beloved country and warned against the dangers of totalitarianism. Only free men could make Russia successful in the modern world. "We must," he wrote, "have love of work which comes from freedom."

Mendeleyev died in St. Petersburg in January of 1907. A procession of thousands followed his coffin through the snowy streets of St. Petersburg to the church of the Technological Institute and then to Volkovo Cemetery. Students carried under their arms the *Principles of Chemistry*. A tablet bearing the Periodic Table was placed upon the grave.

The fame of the great Siberian endures. The Mendeleyev Institute has become, over the years, Russia's largest center for training chemists. Updated versions of the Periodic Table appear in textbooks and hang on classroom walls around the world.

Glen Seaborg, Nobel Prize-winning American chemist, has said, "Mendeleyev's Periodic system to this day serves as the basis for subtlest and most complex researches. Therefore, Mendeleyev's name will, in the future, too, continue to be eternalized by new and yet newer discoveries of synthesized elements and by unlocking of new and yet newer secrets of nature."

Chapter VII
Louis Pasteur
One Who Performed Miracles

The sciences are not tidy fields separated one from the other by "no trespassing" signs and high fences. The fences are, in fact, low. Some scientists straddle them, others go leap-frogging over.

Louis Pasteur was one who went leap-frogging from chemistry to physics to biology to medicine, finding treasures everywhere. The walls of the Parisian chapel in which he is buried are decorated with nine mosaics, each illustrating a field of science to which he made a major contribution.

Louis Pasteur was born on December 27, 1822, in the village of Dôle in eastern France. His father, Jean Joseph, was a hard-working tanner who processed animal hides into supple leather. The boy's early memories were of the pungent odor of hides smeared with dung and of the brown dye of the tanning vats.

But Jean Joseph had known days of glory. He had been a soldier in the conquering army of the Emperor Napoleon. Napoleon himself had pinned on his shoulder the red ribbon of the Legion of Honor awarded for bravery in battle. With his idol defeated by the British, Jean Joseph still wore his medal. He was deeply patriotic and impressed on his son an ardent belief in the greatness of France, Empire, Kingdom or Republic.

Jean Joseph was a man with little education but a thirst for learning. He was determined that his son would rise in the world. Louis must become a teacher, perhaps even the headmaster of a school.

True, the boy was not an outstanding student but he was industrious, patient and quiet. Nobody would ever accuse Louis Pasteur of being an idle chatterbox.

Always he set high standards for himself. When he applied for entrance to the École Normale Supérieure, the Parisian college for training teachers, he was accepted but did not rank high enough in the entrance examinations to satisfy himself. He spent a further year of preparation, scored better on the examinations and so went off to Paris to immerse himself in his studies, especially in chemistry.

Jean Joseph wrote to his son many letters of advice. Louis was not to study so hard that he damaged his health. He was not to go out in the dangerous streets of Paris alone and he was to return home early. At night he should not go out at all. He was to read plays in his own room rather than attend live theater. At the first sign of a cold, he was to dose himself carefully and he must take two or three not-too-warm baths each week.

Louis, for his part, wrote equally earnest advice to his sisters at home. Sometimes he suspected, sadly, that his advice was having little effect on the girls. Still he went on in "not a few letters," as he himself confessed, to tell them that, if they once tried hard work, they would find it very enjoyable. Certainly they were to read the good books he sent them. Above all, they were not to squabble and slap each other so much.

In the meantime, Louis himself was growing ever and ever more engrossed in the world of science. He went to exciting chemistry lectures, often arriving half an hour early to be sure of a seat. Soon he persuaded a distinguished professor to let him become his teaching assistant.

Pasteur's first original research was in the field of

crystals, a popular topic at the time. Most chemical compounds can appear in crystal form, he learned, and each crystal of a given compound has its own characteristic shape, unlike that of any other. The crystals of quartz, for example, are six-sided. The crystals of common table salt are perfect cubes with, of course, six faces. Other crystals have far more complicated shapes with varying numbers of faces.

Pasteur soon observed that crystals of the same compounds are not always symmetrical. Some are what the French chemist Biot had called "right-handed", some "left-handed." They are, in other words, mirror images. Crystals affect beams of light shining through them. They cause light to appear to the human eye in what scientists call "a plane of polarization." Right-handed crystals deflect that plane to the right, left-handed crystals deflect it to the left.

Surprising to Pasteur in the mid-nineteenth century was the discovery that some compounds, when dissolved into the liquid form, continue to deflect light. Others in liquid form do not deflect at all.

It was a mystery which the young Pasteur could not resist. He did much patient research with a new instrument called the polarimeter measuring the diffractions of polarized light. But he did not stop there. He designed experiments which proved that not only were some crystals asymmetrical, the molecules that made up those crystals were asymmetrical, also. So was born the new field of stereo-chemistry, the study of the way atoms are arranged inside molecules.

For Pasteur the universe itself was disymmetrical, that is, made up of two kinds of symmetry. Was it this disymmetry which had created life in the world, he asked himself. He would never be able to prove so bold a conjecture, but he would always remember with wistful affection his early research.

In the meantime, he had completed his studies at the École Normale in 1846. Graduates were expected to spend ten years teaching wherever in France the Ministry of Education sent them. But Pasteur longed to continue his own research. For a time he was allowed to stay in Paris as a laboratory assistant. Later he was appointed teacher of physics at a high school in Dijon. Soon, however, friends, who recognized his gifts, were able to have him sent as a chemistry professor to the University of Strasbourg.

With other newcomers, Pasteur was invited to a reception given by the rector of the university. There he met the rector's blue-eyed daughter Marie. Two weeks later the rector received an astonishing letter from the young chemist. In it Pasteur detailed his modest but honorable family background. He detailed also his own future prospects as a research scientist, and he announced that his father would soon come to Strasbourg to ask that Louis be granted Marie's hand in marriage! As was the custom, Louis wrote to Mademoiselle Marie, herself, later. He only wished he were more worthy, but he had a heart full of love for her, he said.

Though so swiftly, Pasteur was convinced that he had found everything he had wanted in a wife. He was right. The marriage took place in May. Pasteur returned to his laboratory and his crystals. Marie set about learning to understand her husband's work and to protect his genius.

Although a young professor earned a low salary, Pasteur used much of the prize money he received buying not household necessities but laboratory equipment. For many years he worked fifteen hours a day. He was no conversationalist, talking very little, either in the laboratory or at home. Marie understood that his truest companions were the ideas teeming in his head. She must often have been lonely, but her husband's remarkable achievements would, in the end, seem also to be her own.

When he was thirty-two years old, Pasteur became professor of chemistry and dean of the science faculty at the University of Lille in northern France. Lille was a busy industrial city. There Pasteur took his students out of the laboratory to visit factories and to learn what they could contribute as chemists. He himself appeared to turn from the "pure science" which had been his delight to the solution of practical problems. Yet always for him, the solution of a practical problem advanced the basic understanding of nature. "There are no such things as pure and applied science — there are only science and the applications of science," he said.

In 1856, a Lille factory owner named Bigo came to the young professor for help. Bigo manufactured alcohol from beet sugar. The alcohol was much needed for industrial purposes, but the company had a serious problem. For months most of its alcohol had spoiled. What to do?

Very soon, Marie Pasteur was writing wryly to her father-in-law in Arbois. "Louis.... was up to his neck in beet juice."

It has sometimes been said that, as a scientist, Pasteur had amazingly good luck. He himself declared that "chance favors the prepared mind." He studied his chosen problems so extensively that when he went to his microscope he knew what he wanted to see. Looking patiently and thoughtfully, he often found what other people had missed.

Now he looked at fermenting beet juice. The process of fermentation breaks down all organic or living matter which contains starch or sugar. Pasteur would later say "all living beings are ferments under certain conditions of their lives." Sugar-containing plants like grapes, barley, hops and beets, if left alone for a time, begin to bubble or ferment. The cause of this fermentation was hotly debated in Pasteur's day. Von Liebig, the great German chemist, thought the process was a chemical reaction. No, said Pasteur, only living organisms could be the cause.

Other scientists had already seen under the microscope tiny "animalcules" which moved and grew and clearly had life. They had found the spherical, one-celled plants of yeast. In Monsieur Bigo's beet juice, Pasteur found just such globules.

But he noticed that, when the alcohol began to spoil, the spherical yeast cells began to grow longer. When fermentation was far advanced, the organisms were very long. Very importantly, also, he noticed that the cells of yeast were not the only micro-organisms present in Monsieur Bigo's alcohol. There was a host of other, even smaller, organisms which must cause the spoilage.

Voilá! Monsieur Bigo must have said. My answer! Pasteur's simple advice to check the progress of the fermentation process allowed the manufacturer to avoid many of the failures he had known.

The basic problem was, of course, far more complicated. Pasteur, with his passionate curiosity, continued to seek answers to the questions his own work had raised.

In 1857, he returned to Paris to become director of scientific studies and administrator at his alma mater, the École Normale. Although he was happy to be back in the center of French scientific life, no splendid laboratory awaited him there. At first he worked alone without assistants in two small attic rooms, making much of his own apparatus. Only gradually he was given more help and allowed a larger space. Even then he was obliged to keep the trays in which he grew his pure ferments under a stairway where he must go on hands and knees to observe them.

Pasteur's work on beet juice and industrial alcohol soon led him to work on other kinds of fermentation. Many scientists believed that living matter could be created out of dead or non-living matter. Spontaneous generation this mysterious process was called. Over the centuries, many people had believed that flies and maggots were born of rotting meat. Mice could be bred by storing a dirty shirt in a bin with wheat or cheese. Aristotle had said that frogs and salamanders grew from slime.

By Pasteur's time most scientists were willing to admit that creatures big enough to be seen by the naked eye were not created *de novo* but had been produced by living parents like themselves. In the teeming world of organisms to be seen only under a microscope, however, many leading authorities claimed creation worked differently. Spontaneous generation took place, they said.

Always imaginative but always cautious, Pasteur never claimed that spontaneous generation had <u>never</u> taken place. He did claim, after a series of long and exhaustive experiments, that he had never observed it. Even today, no one is certain how life began on our planet or whether, in some far distant future, human inventions will one day be able to reproduce themselves. But Pasteur was able to prove that, for all practical purposes and under normal conditions, spontaneous generation does not happen upon Earth. "Life is a germ," said Pasteur, "and a germ is life."

His proof was accomplished by means as simple as those John Dalton had used in the Lake District in England. With a mule to carry his flasks of sterilized water, he climbed high into the Alps and found, as he expected, that in that unpolluted air the water in his open flasks remained pure. In dust-laden farm country the microbes in the air quickly invaded the water in his flasks.

As years went by, he would do research on the fermentation and diseases of vinegar, wine, beer, cheese and souring milk. He would make the important discovery that heating these liquids to a degree suitable for each would destroy the micro-organisms which could cause disease or early spoilage. This heating process, soon known and used around the world, would be named pasteurization after its discoverer. Pasteur took out patents on his process for treating wine and milk but gave those patents free to the public. In his view, the nation which devoted itself the most whole-heartedly to science would be the strongest and bring the most good to its people. He intended to do his part to advance the strength of France.

His work, his country and his family were Pasteur's life-long passions. He and Marie had five children whom he loved dearly. Three of the five died in childhood, victims of sicknesses for which there were then no cures. The stricken father's answer to grief was to work harder and harder.

In 1865, another great French industry appealed to him for help. The silk worms which spun the fine thread for France's famous silk cloth were falling ill. The unhealthy worms were chewing their way through their own cocoons, making the thread useless for weaving upon the once-busy looms of Lyons, France's second city. Thousands of men and women were out of work and hungry.

Even Pasteur was taken aback by the challenge offered him. "I have never touched a silk worm," he admitted. But he did not hesitate for long. As usual, he read everything he could find in this new field. Then he went south to Pont Gisquet with his assistants, his wife and his eight-year-old daughter, Marie Louise.

In the warm and sunny world of Provence, orange and olive trees thrived as did the mulberry tree, the "tree of gold", whose leaves were the only food of the growing silk worms. All of Pasteur's company, including small Marie Louise, set about raising silk worms and collecting and selecting healthy eggs. Marie Louise even learned to use a microscope for this painstaking study.

Nature often surprises eager researchers. Pasteur and his assistants discovered that there were two silk worm diseases. These were caused by micro-organisms which could be detected in the silk moth's body. In order to stop the epidemic all infected moths should be destroyed. Not every breeder was willing to adopt this drastic system overnight, but gradually most were convinced. Silk worm disease was soon greatly reduced. The Pasteurs could go back to Paris.

Madame Pasteur and Marie Louise may not have been glad to leave lovely Provence for the stern, almost monastic life at the Pasteur apartment in the École Normale. That life had, in fact, developed problems having little to do with science.

Pasteur was a revolutionary in science but a conservative in society. A soldier's son, he believed in discipline and obedience. In the nineteenth century, French governments changed frequently. Sometimes the country was a Republic, sometimes it fell under Imperial rule. Pasteur cheered for the first short-lived Republic, but he easily became a supporter of the Emperor Napoleon III, nephew of the great Bonaparte who had honored his father.

Little interested in politics, Pasteur believed that Frenchmen should be loyal to the government in power. He had no sympathy for young people who defied the Emperor and, as director of the École Normale, he expelled ardent student defenders of free speech. In the midst of the resulting controversy, he resigned his position and became instead professor of chemistry at the University of Paris.

Perhaps, after all, he was relieved. Research would always be his passion. He would never quite understand people who had other concerns. Even a severe stroke when he was forty-five years old could not keep him from his ponderings and his experiments. The illness damaged the left side of his body. It did not affect his brilliant mind.

The Franco-Prussian War forced him for a time from his Parisian laboratory. It also sent him and Marie on a frantic carriage ride through fleeing French troops in a successful search for their soldier son. In 1871 at the war's end, the family returned to Paris and to what was to become Pasteur's greatest fame.

He no longer had any doubt that microbes caused fermentation and its opposite, putrefaction, or decay. He did not doubt that microbes were present everywhere except in the pure air on the highest mountain peaks. Out of fear of infection he was himself immensely careful about what he touched.

But was his caution justified? Did microbes actually cause disease in large animals and in human beings? Though few yet agreed with him, Pasteur had come to think so. He decided further that contagious diseases were spread by microbes. Since this was true, there must be some way to prevent such diseases.

Jenner, a country doctor in England in the late 1700's, had found a way to guard his patients against the often fatal disease smallpox. He scratched matter from a smallpox sore into the skin of a boy who had had the similar but far milder rash known as cowpox. The boy stayed healthy. Jenner's vaccination had, by the 1870's, won wide acclaim.

Pasteur began his own vaccination experiments with animals. First he attacked chicken cholera whose bacteria had already been identified. By what may have been a happy accident, broth containing cholera bacteria was left standing for some days in the laboratory before being injected into chickens. The bacteria had grown weak with time. The chickens fell ill but recovered. When they later received the injection of a virulent broth of cholera bacteria, they did not catch the disease. Pasteur and his co-workers had found a valuable vaccine.

Pasteur turned next to anthrax, a serious sickness of cows and sheep. A fresh surprise! Anthrax bacteria did not behave like those of chicken cholera. Standing in a broth, they did not grow less virulent. Instead, they formed spores which were microscopic, dormant stages of bacteria, hard to destroy. After much patient experimentation, the difficulty was overcome by heating spores to 107.6 degrees Fahrenheit, thus killing the disease-bearing bacteria. Pasteur could offer yet another vaccine to the farmers of France. The demand was so immediate and so great that laboratory technicians sometimes grew tired and made minor mistakes in preparation, but that problem was overcome. By 1894, nearly a million-and-a-half sheep and hundreds of thousands of cattle had been successfully vaccinated.

Pasteur himself was by now seriously unwell and no longer young. Much of his work was being performed by the helping hands of brilliant assistants. Yet he still felt what has been called his "longing for romantic problems." He accepted one final challenge, *la rage* — rabies! Anyone unlucky enough to be bitten by a rabid animal was almost certain to die a terrible death. No one knew the cause of the disease. Certainly no one had a cure.

With his assistants, Pasteur began one last, long, and patient set of experiments. As always, there were some set-backs, but in the end he decided that a tiny organism, which could not be seen under a microscope — a virus it is called today — was the carrier of rabies. He found no cure for the disease. A hundred years later there is still no cure. He did, however, with his assistants, develop a vaccine using the dried spinal cords of infected rabbits. A series of injections of these infected cords in liquid prevented dogs who had been bitten by rabid animals from developing the disease.

Dogs could be saved, yes. But people? How could even

Pasteur be sure? There had been no experiments on human beings.

One day, in 1885, Pasteur was presented with a terrible choice. A nine-year-old Alsatian boy appeared in his laboratory. Two days before, Joseph Meister had been bitten fourteen times by a rabid dog. His mother implored the great scientist to use the new rabies vaccine on her son. Everyone knew that the vaccine was untried. It might do nothing to prevent the boy's sickness. It might even kill him. On the other hand, it might save his life.

After profound soul-searching and consultation with physicians, Pasteur ordered that the vaccine be tried. Joseph Meister lived! In adulthood he would become a janitor at the great Pasteur Institute. So deep was his gratitude that when the German armies captured Paris during World War II, Meister killed himself rather than open Pasteur's tomb to the foreign invaders.

Despite his success, some scientists and doctors sharply criticized Pasteur for using an untried treatment on a living person. The general public did not quibble. People came from all over Europe and from America to be vaccinated. They and the animals needed for production of the vaccine crowded the laboratories where Pasteur visited and eagerly watched over them. He had a few sad failures. Some patients reached Paris too late to forestall the dread sickness, but many, many lives were saved.

Pasteur had won his final and most dramatic victory.

By now, honors and prizes of many kinds had been showered upon him. He continued always his austere lifestyle. The monument which truly mattered to him was the splendid Pasteur Institute which opened in 1888, financed by donors from around the world.

Pasteur died in Paris in 1895. He was buried at his Institute with a lavish State funeral, a tanner's son, honored by the most distinguished of his fellow citizens.

This naturally quiet, often taciturn man fought many public battles throughout his long, professional life. "I did not know I had so many enemies," he once said. He did refuse a challenge to a duel, but he could not resist answering all verbal attacks. In letters, articles, lectures and dramatic demonstrations, he confronted his foes. All in the name of science, he insisted. "I am armed for combat, struggle and victory."

Some of Pasteur's opponents were noted fellow scientists like the Germans von Liebig and Robert Koch. Koch declared that Pasteur took credit for work that he himself had done.

Other enemies were like the critical but unwise Marquis who, so Pasteur informed him in a witty letter, had read only a very few of the master's papers and had not understood those few!

Some of his opponents were French scientists jealous of Pasteur's ability to attract funds for his research. Some ordinary citizens objected to the kennel of stray and rabid dogs which he set up in their neighborhood. Anti-vivisectionists, as animal rights activists were called in the nineteenth century, protested his free use of animals for his experiments. Manufacturers sometimes resented lectures from "a mere chemist." Angry physicians could not believe that they themselves carried disease to their patients on unwashed hands and garments.

Time has proved that in a few of his battles Pasteur was wrong. In most, he was triumphantly correct.

His son-in-law, René Vallery-Radot, and his daughter, the Marie Louise who had as a small girl helped to tend her father's silk worms, devoted their own lives to collecting Pasteur's voluminous papers and to preserving his memory.

An envelope addressed simply "To the one who

performs miracles" was once dropped into a French mailbox. The postal service delivered the envelope to Pasteur's door.

The "miracles" had been performed by a lifetime of arduous effort. "When I spend a day away from my work, I feel that I have been a thief," Pasteur said.

Today the Pasteur Institute remains at the forefront in research on human diseases, including the scourge of the late twentieth century, AIDS.

Chapter VIII
Marie and Irène Curie
Chemists of the Invisible

To be a child of conquered and unhappy Poland. To be nervous and shy. To be poor. Most serious of all, to be a girl. These were the roadblocks which fate placed in the path of Manya Sklodowska.

The little girl was born in November 1867 in a crowded Warsaw apartment on cobbled Freta Street. She was the youngest child of impoverished school teacher parents who passionately longed for the independence of their native land even as they struggled to support their family and to avoid offending Poland's ruthless Russian masters.

These good parents quickly noticed that their timid Manya was precocious. She could read at four with only her six-year-old sister Bronia as her teacher. At school she recited her lessons in perfectly-accented Russian to satisfy the inspector who must not know that classes were secretly taught in Polish. In her family's tiny apartment, constantly changing with her parents' shifting fortunes, four noisy siblings could not distract her from her beloved books and her own thoughts.

Such a bright and earnest little girl could expect to grow up to be a school teacher like her adored mother. She could not hope for her father's modest university training in mathematics and physics. Universities in both Poland and Russia were closed to women.

Tragedy came early to the Sklodowski family. When Manya was nine years old, her oldest sister died of typhus contracted from pupils their father housed and tutored. Two years later, Madame Sklodowska died of tuberculosis after a long illness during which she dared not touch her children for fear of infecting them.

Even in sorrow, Manya's father was determined that his children must be well-educated. What must matter for them was the life of the mind.

Only a few months after her mother's death, Manya was sent to a strict government *gymnasium*. Russians dominated this high school where it was rumored that clever Polish students were deliberately failed. The Czar of all the Russias did not want to educate a Polish generation which might rise against him.

But even the most hostile of her teachers could not deny young Manya's brilliance. She excelled in all her subjects. When she graduated at fifteen she was awarded the gold medal for being first in her class. Her older brother and her sister Bronia had won gold medals before her. She must have resolved to equal them.

Two years younger than her classmates, she was not yet old enough to plan for the future. Her wise father sent her off to the countryside to visit relatives. Poles believed strongly in the value of country life. Manya herself was always to love the countryside.

Now she was caught up in what turned out to be the most carefree year of her life. It was a sixteen-year-old's dream time. There were lively cousins, uncles and aunts, merry sleigh rides over glistening snow and night-long dances with romantic waltzes and vigorous mazurkas. Manya boasted in her letters to a Warsaw friend about the handsome young men from Cracow who queued up to claim her as a partner. In the midst of such excitement she was reading only "harmless little books" and had abandoned her embroidery altogether!

The merry days did not last. Back in Warsaw, with her loyal but ever poorer father, Manya's natural love of learning returned. While she tried to earn money as a children's tutor, she herself became a student at a floating university for women. The daring school held secret classes in many parts of the city, often in small private apartments. Dedicated teachers risked their own safety to teach young women otherwise denied an education.

But the floating university was not enough. Soon Manya and her sister Bronia, always her dearest friend, began to yearn for study in France. They would attend the Sorbonne, the great University of Paris, to which for 700 years students and professors had come from all over Europe. An impossible dream? The Sklodowska sisters made a pact. Bronia, the older, who wanted to become a doctor like the girls' brother, would go to Paris first. Manya would stay in Poland, work and send money. When her own studies were complete, the older sister would help the younger.

For the next five years, the younger sister worked as tutor and governess, sometimes happily, sometimes with an aching heart. As always shy but intense, she fell deeply in love with the handsome older brother of two of her pupils. Her employers forbade their son's marriage to a penniless governess and the young man, perhaps regretfully, obeyed them.

Manya fought her pain. She would never let herself be beaten down by persons or events, she decided. Once more teaching in Warsaw, she returned to classes at the floating university and began to study chemistry.

At last on a day in 1890 after so many years of waiting, a crucial letter arrived from Paris. Bronia was about to be married. She and her medical student husband offered Manya lodging in their apartment.

So, in 1891, frightened as she was, a plump young Polish

woman with curly ash-blond hair and sober gray eyes purchased a third-class railroad ticket for the French capital. There at the Sorbonne she registered as Mademoiselle Marie Sklodowska.

Unfortunately, the newly-christened Marie, who thought she knew French well, found it hard to follow lectures. She herself spoke French with a strong Polish accent which made her fellow students laugh. Her scientific background, especially in mathematics, was poor. To add to her difficulties, Bronia lived an hour's ride by horse-drawn bus from the university. What was more, her sister's suburban apartment was a lively center for young Poles in Paris. The apartment was great fun but not a helpful place for an ill-prepared student with a burning determination to excel.

After a few months, Marie moved to a garret room in a sober stone apartment building only a few moments' walk from the Sorbonne. Now she could devote herself day and night to her studies.

Soon she cut off nearly all personal relationships except with her sister and brother-in-law. She had become a lone voyager, an eager explorer in the world of science.

Walking between her garret room and the Sorbonne laboratories, Marie was bothered not at all by the fact that in Paris of the 1890's young women who valued their reputation went out into the streets only with carefully-chosen escorts. She was bothered not at all by the writer, Octave Mirabeau, who said that "woman is not a brain, she is a sex."

In the last years of the nineteenth century, twelve thousand students were enrolled at the University of Paris. Marie, like many students, was poor. Coal was expensive. On cold winter nights she piled all her clothes on top of her blankets to keep herself warm. Her only stove was a small alcohol lamp. Meals were usually "bread with a cup of chocolate, eggs or fruit." Sometimes she hardly ate at all. The plump figure of her girlhood slipped away. For the rest of her life she would be slender and delicate.

In 1893, Mademoiselle Marie Sklodowska received her *Licence es Sciences Physiques*, the equivalent of a Master's degree in Physics. She was the first women ever to be awarded this degree. In a class of thirty her examination paper took first place. A year later, helped by scholarship money from Poland, she received a *Licence es Sciences Mathématiques*, this time taking second place.

The degrees would assure a teaching position in Poland. Marie had always intended to return to help her unhappy country. Bronia would, in time, go back and with her husband set up a mountain sanitorium for tuberculosis patients. In Warsaw, Marie's father, now somewhat more prosperous, had taken an apartment where his youngest daughter could live with him.

Yet for all of her love for her country and her family, Marie hesitated. It was not the modest assignment of studying the magnetism of different kinds of steel, an opportunity offered her by France's Society for the Encouragement of National Industry, which held her.

Something of greater importance had happened. Early in 1894, Marie had met Pierre Curie. She never forgot her first glimpse of him. Tall, red-haired with a short, pointed beard and dreamer's eyes, he stood outlined against a French window.

Pierre Curie was unique among the fine scientists Marie had met in France. He was an outsider to the elite scientific world. A shy and awkward boy who needed to sink deeply into a single subject, not move glibly from field to field, he had been tutored at home. He had never attended one of the *grandes écoles*, the well-known French *lycées*. He was not interested in honors, degrees and competition. Though he had published outstanding papers on magnetism and crystals, he had never troubled to finish his Ph.D. degree. He was dedicated to "pure science," the pursuit of knowledge for its own sake.

At 35, with all his brilliance, Pierre held only a poorly-paid post as the laboratory chief and instructor at the new and ill-equipped EPCI, the municipal school of industrial physics and chemistry. He had vowed to lead a monk-like life.

That vow Pierre now speedily abandoned. Friends had introduced Marie to him in the hope that he could offer her laboratory space at the EPCI. He soon offered her something else, a life together devoted to pure science. After months of indecision, Marie accepted. On July 26, 1895, the two were married at the town hall in Sceaux, the pretty wooded suburb where Pierre's parents lived and where he had spent a happy, secluded boyhood.

With wedding gift money, the newlyweds purchased bicycles, then the rage of forward-looking Parisians who even suggested that the bicycle might liberate women. The Curies set off to explore Brittany, immersing themselves in the natural world which both loved.

Pierre had by now, perhaps at Marie's urging, completed his Ph.D. and obtained an EPCI professorship. His salary was still small, and to help with family finances Marie took a year's course to qualify as a science instructor in a teacher training school for girls. In 1896, her first child, Irène, was born. Marie adored her baby and recorded with scientific precision all the details of Irène's progress.

But motherhood could never be her whole life. Interior decoration and gourmet cookery were to play no part at all. The Curies' apartment was sparsely furnished, their food was plain.

Two years after her marriage, Marie began work on her

Ph.D., that chance to pursue "pure science" which Pierre had offered when he courted her. No woman in Europe had yet received a Ph.D. in science but Marie was unconcerned.

A Sorbonne Ph.D. required that a candidate do original research. Seeking a challenging problem, Marie turned to a new, exciting, even mysterious field.

In 1896, the year of Irène's birth, a German physicist named Wilhelm Roentgen, was travelling about western Europe demonstrating x-rays to astonished audiences. Nobody could understand these newly-discovered rays. What everyone could see was what they did. They caused certain minerals to glow, in some cases very strongly. They exposed photographic plates. They penetrated wood and metal, even human flesh.

Roentgen had produced a notable photograph which showed the bone structure of his wife's hand and the ring upon her finger. Frau Roentgen was dismayed. Was there no privacy?

It is claimed that modest ladies grew fearful that scientists would now peer at them through the brick walls of their homes. But doctors, undismayed, very soon began using x-rays to determine breaks in the bones of their patients.

Roentgen had made his discovery while experimenting with cathode tubes. These newly invented glass tubes, evacuated to a near perfect vacuum, contained two electric terminals, the cathode and the anode. An electric current caused a glowing line from cathode to anode to appear. That the glow was caused by electrifying the trace of gas in the imperfectly-evacuated tube would be gradually realized. Roentgen himself wanted to know how far the rays created in this way could move outside the glass walls of the cathode tube and how thick a barrier they could penetrate.

The results of his experiments had obvious practical

results and not for medical diagnosis alone. Scientists around the world began their own researches into the uses and nature of x-rays.

Marie Curie might well have done her own research in this fashionable field but Marie was never concerned with fashion. She chose to follow up on the obscure work of Henri Becquerel whom Roentgen's x-rays had inspired. Becquerel was a distinguished Parisian professor, a member of the elite Academy of Science, son and grandson of noted researchers in the field of phosphorescence.

Phosphorescence is the radiance, or glow, which light excites in certain substances. That radiance persists for some time after the light has been turned off. Fluorescence is the glow which results when certain substances absorb light of one color or wave-length and give off light of another color or wave-length. Fluorescence does not continue when the exciting light is turned off.

It occurred to Henri Becquerel, learning of Roentgen's work, that phosphorescent and fluorescent substances might also produce x-rays under intense sunlight. He set about experimenting with samples of wood and stone collected over the years by his father and grandfather. To his disappointment only one of the samples had any effect on photographic plates. Salts of the element uranium did produce an impression on a photographic plate. Unexpectedly, sunlight was not necessary to the phenomenon. Uranium salt placed in a dark cupboard for several days also "took a picture." Becquerel's first startling experiment produced the image of a thin copper cross which he had inserted between the uranium and the black paper covering a photographic plate.

Light obviously did not cause the radiation. The invisible rays must be emitted by the uranium itself. How was this possible? Everything physicists and chemists had believed about the nature of matter seemed contradicted.

Becquerel performed and reported on a few more experiments but his fellow scientists did not respond. Gradually he himself lost interest in his own curious findings. Perhaps those findings were too controversial and uncomfortable. Besides, uranium did not produce good bone pictures. X-rays did a far better job. Also, the equipment for producing x-rays, a vacuum tube and a high-voltage coil, was cheap and easily available. Uranium was very hard to obtain.

Enough reasons for neglect. That neglect was the very reason Marie Curie, seeking a research project, settled upon what she herself would later call "radioactivity." The field was completely new. Except for Becquerel's few brief papers, nothing had been written about it. Marie would not need to assemble a tiresome bibliography of references. She could get to work at once.

Providing, of course, that she could find a laboratory!

No well-equipped laboratories were available. Pierre himself, though a professor, had had to perform experiments in crowded school halls. Now with his help and encouragement, Marie was grateful to be assigned first to a small room at the School of Physics, later to an abandoned shed once used by medical students for dissecting cadavers.

The high-ceilinged room was unheated, the floor was earthen, the roof leaked so that experiments would have to be set up where raindrops would not fall. There was no venting for noxious fumes. But there were space and quiet. There were work tables and soon there were the remarkable instruments which Pierre provided or created new, in part out of wooden grocery crates, to measure the electrical energy or "ionizing current" of the Becquerel rays.

Marie began with measuring the energy emitted by uranium powder given her by a colleague. After that, she set about scavenging for a variety of samples. Gold, silver, other familiar elements all went into her "condensation chamber." Like Becquerel, she found that, except for uranium, these elements emitted no rays or "nothing clear."

Then, on February 17, 1898, she tested a sample of the dark and lustrous mineral compound called pitchblende. Pitchblende was mined in the St. Joachimstahl region on the German-Czech border. It was of practical interest largely because it contained uranium. Uranium itself was of industrial interest largely because it was used in glass-making.

To Marie's astonishment, pitchblende, heated and treated chemically, produced an electrical current much stronger than that given off by pure uranium.

It must be, Marie and Pierre decided, that pitchblende contained, in addition to uranium, radioactive elements which no one had known before. Throughout the nineteenth century, chemists had been busy adding new elements to Mendeleyev's Periodic Table. That radioactivity might be a method of discovering yet more new elements was a stunning idea. It was an idea which Marie and Pierre together set about proving in the laboratory, Pierre as physicist, Marie as chemist.

Persuaded by painstaking chemical treatments and distillations, they announced that pitchblende, which gave off such strong radiation, contained, in addition to uranium, not one but two mystery elements which were radioactive. The Curies named these new elements polonium, after Marie's native Poland, and radium, derived from the Latin word for rays.

It was true that conventional tests did not support the Curies' claim, yet many scientists were ready to believe them. Marie was determined to provide unassailable proof.

For four years she worked in her cold and leaky shed to

extract pure radium from pitchblende. The St. Joachimstahl mines shipped to Paris over ten tons of their "waste" ore from which the valuable uranium had been extracted. The Curies paid the railroad charges from their own small savings. The great glistening masses arrived in sacks at the shed on the rue Lhomond still mixed with dust and pine needles from the forest into which they had been tossed.

Perhaps even stubborn Marie would not have undertaken her task if she had known that in all her cauldrons filled with bubbling pitchblende there was only one-millionth part of radium. There was something else she could not know — the danger posed by the radioactive substances to herself and others. As she worked, her fingertips became painful and deeply scarred. Both she and Pierre suffered burns which healed only slowly. Even Henri Becquerel, to his indignation, was unexpectedly burned by a radioactive fragment carried in his coat pocket.

The Curies seem never to have taken these warnings seriously nor did they connect their own periods of bad health and Pierre's ever-growing weakness with radioactivity. They were supremely happy in their research and found special joy, when night ended their exhausting days, in admiring the soft blue glow of their samples.

In 1902, Marie announced that she had isolated one-tenth of a gram, roughly one-three-hundredths of an ounce, of the white shiny metal, pure radium. It did exist. It could be weighed and measured.

Marie and Pierre refused to patent their extraction process. A patent could have made them fabulously rich since radium was soon in great demand, recognized for its ability to fight cancer. Like Louis Pasteur, the Curies believed that science made a nation great and that scientific knowledge belonged to all the people.

Marie had come to a startling conclusion about

Becquerel's mysterious rays. They were not related to Roentgen's x-rays, though x-rays had inspired Becquerel's first research. Becquerel's rays, those upon which she and Pierre worked, were the result of atomic action. The stable and indivisible atom, sturdy building block of matter which John Dalton had described and Jacob Berzelius supported, was a myth. The nuclei, or centers, of some atoms were not immutable. They were constantly changing, giving off radiation as they changed. It would soon be discovered, in fact, that radioactive elements were in the process of disappearing as they gave birth to other elements, uranium, to radium, to radon and more.

By now researchers in many laboratories were excitedly working in this new field. The Curies were widely recognized.

Pierre received a long hoped for appointment at the University of Paris. Marie was offered a paying job at Sèvres, a training school for future teachers. In 1903, she received her Ph.D., *très honorables*, the first woman in France to earn a doctorate. In that same year, Pierre, Marie and Becquerel were awarded the Nobel Prize in physics, another first for a woman. The money from this and other prizes, though generously shared, freed the Curies from their extreme poverty. The prize also brought fame and attention which deeply distressed the shy couple.

A far deeper distress awaited Marie.

On a dark and rainy day in 1906, Pierre, who had long been troubled by weakness in his legs, slipped beneath the wheels of a horse-drawn carriage on a busy Parisian street. He died at once, his skull crushed.

At 36, Marie was left alone to raise Irène and Ève, their second daughter, just three years old. For that task she had the help of Polish governesses and Pierre's father. Old Dr. Curie especially delighted in the grave little Irène who was clearly destined to become a scientist like her parents.

Other tasks Marie faced alone—continuing the research she and Pierre had begun, working to create the Radium Institute of which he had dreamed, accepting the professorship he had held. A fragile, black-clad figure, she became the first woman ever to lecture at the Sorbonne. She began her first class with the simple phrase "when one considers progress that has been made in physics during the past ten years." The words started exactly where Pierre had left off in his lesson plan. Marie had long since decided that a great reserve was the only wise course for a woman as emotional as she knew herself to be.

She showed the same outer control in 1911 when, as a woman, she was denied membership in the Academy of Science. No woman had ever been elected to the Academy. Men thought Marie impudent to apply.

Overall, 1911 was to be a tumultuous year. Marie was accused of having a love affair with a married colleague. The Parisian press attacked her as a "foreign woman" and home-wrecker. But in 1911, also, she was awarded the Nobel Prize in chemistry for her discovery of polonium and radium.

Nothing stopped her work. Marie fought for a Radium Institute, planned it, oversaw its construction, even planted the trees in its garden. In 1914, the fine new building separated by a newly-planted garden from the great Pasteur Institute was nearly ready for use. But as so often in a life during which illness interrupted health, and sorrow canceled joy, Marie was faced with a new monster. World War I! A German invasion threatened.

The beautiful city of Paris with its countless architectural treasures fell silent. Many Parisians fled. Marie must watch over her Institute and a precious gram of radium which must not fall into German hands.

When she had carried the treasure in its leaden box south to Bordeaux for safety, she returned to Paris. She could do nothing to help her native Poland which was now occupied by Germans. She could help the wounded soldiers of the French army.

X-rays were now regularly used in the U.S. and elsewhere for the detection of broken bones and foreign objects in the human body. The French army had no x-ray equipment. Marie set up stations of radiology. She outfitted an ordinary touring car with radiologic equipment, together with a dynamo for producing the necessary electric current. She herself, with a driver, carried her valuable equipment to the doctors and their suffering patients. Because of her urging, many "little Curies", other radiologic cars, were soon going within a mile or two of the front where the French and German armies clashed.

In this work Marie's principal helper was her seventeen-year-old daughter, Irène. Irene, a brilliant girl who had already earned her *Licence es Sciences Physiques*, like her mother traveled to the battlefields with radiologic equipment and in Paris trained new operators. Gradually also the two women, together with Marie's only remaining laboratory assistant, moved equipment from Pierre's old rooms to the new and still silent laboratories at the Radium Institute. They must be ready to carry on the research which the terrible war had interrupted.

World War I ended at last in 1918. Marie's beloved Poland became a free and independent country. Ignace Paderewski, the penniless young pianist whom she had met long ago in her sister Bronia's Parisian apartment, became Poland's first president.

In 1918, also, Marie, as director, officially opened the Radium Institute of the University of Paris.

France, though victorious in war, was still too poor

adequately to finance research. Despite all Marie's painful timidity, she was persuaded to try to raise money. The fragile, dark-clad widow and her story proved irresistible.

Radium, still so difficult to extract, was now used in many ways, wise and unwise. It was priced at a hundred thousand dollars a gram. There were 50 grams in the United States, Marie calculated. She herself, the discoverer, used her own tiny store solely to produce radon pellets for the treatment of cancer. She had none at all for her own research.

In 1921, she sailed for the United States seeking financial support. She returned to France with a gram of the precious metal which she insisted must belong not to her but to the Radium Institute. Later she sailed again for America to raise money for Warsaw's new Radium Institute, directed by her doctor sister, Bronia.

Marie's health was increasingly delicate. Her days as a research scientist were over. As a fund raiser, enabling others, she worked to provide her Institute with the finest available equipment. She also set up scholarships to rescue young scientists from the poverty she herself had once known.

Among the students whom she helped to train, perhaps the most notable were the brilliant and dapper young physicist, Frédéric Joliot, and her own daughter, Irène, who would succeed her as director of the Institute.

Irène was awarded her Ph.D. in 1925. It was now known that in a process of disintegration radioactive elements gave off different kinds of particles — alpha rays, beta rays, gamma rays, all named after letters of the Greek alphabet. Irène's thesis investigated alpha rays emitted by polonium. In 1926, she married Frédéric Joliot, beginning a long and fruitful scientific partnership much like that which Pierre and Marie had more briefly known.

In January 1934, Irène and Frédéric gave Marie what was her last great scientific joy. They bombarded the stable metal aluminum with radium-and polonium-generated particles. Amazingly the aluminum was transformed into radioactive silicon. The Joliot-Curies had discovered artificial radioactivity. Dependence on rare and costly radium in radioactive research was ended. Within the next fifty years some two thousand new radioactive isotopes would be produced.

For their work in synthesizing new radio elements, Irène and Frédéric were awarded the 1935 Nobel Prize in Chemistry. As a fourteen-year-old, Irène had sat in the same room to watch her mother receive the award from the now-aged King of Sweden. This award was a triumph Marie was not to share. She had died the previous July of pernicious anemia. It was a disease almost surely caused by her long exposure to the radiation so beneficial when carefully used, so dangerous when experienced in huge quantities. She was buried quietly at Sceaux in the same grave as her husband.

Like her husband but unlike her mother, Irène Curie took an active interest in the great social causes of her day -feminism, peace, justice for the poor, and, toward the end of her life, elimination of the atomic bomb whose creation the Joliot-Curies' work had unwittingly helped to bring about.

Like her mother, Irène above all else loved her husband, her children and her laboratory. Like her mother, she ignored the precautions which she insisted on for other workers and the signs of radium sickness in her own body.

Twenty-two years after Marie's death, Irène died, a probable victim of the x-rays which as a teen-ager she had carried to wounded soldiers in the trenches of World War I.

She had no complaints. She had led, she declared, "a beautiful life." There had been dark moments of jealousy and misunderstanding and at times deep distrust from fellow scientists who disliked the Joliot-Curies' leftist politics. Irène chose to remember the triumphs.

"In my family," she said simply, "we are accustomed to glory."

A special glory came in 1996 forty years after Irène's death when Marie's and Pierre's ashes in their wooden caskets were carried from the little cemetery at Sceaux to the Panthéon in Paris. Marie Curie became on that day the first woman to be enshrined in France's memorial to the "great men" of her adopted homeland.

Chapter IX

Richard Willstätter
Genius Under Siege

Young Richard Willstätter's distant ancestors had come with the Roman legions to the land which would one day be called Germany, so family legend claimed. In more recent centuries the boy's forefathers had been rabbis and prominent traders and bankers in the city of Augsburg.

In Karlsruhe, where Richard himself was born in 1872, small Jewish boys knew that it was dangerous to go out of their houses alone. Rowdy gangs roamed the streets ready to shout insults and throw stones.

Yet Richard's childhood was happy. He was close friends with his older brother. He and his mother had strong ties which would prove life-long.

Often mother and son walked in the green gardens of the Ducal Palace which stood in the center of town. There the much-respected Grand Duke could often be seen and sometimes greeted.

More daring adventures were the races with the newly-installed horse trolley which made so many stops along lengthy Kaiser Street that a small boy could hope to keep up with it. Best of all were fierce Indian battles in the dark and mysterious Hardt Forest which surrounded Karlsruhe. These battles were inspired by the American James Fenimore Cooper's *Leatherstocking Tales,* which had also delighted Mendeleyev. The warring tribes were led by Richard's brother and his closest friend and included one brave squaw.

School life was pleasant although Richard's mother

thought he did not take his studies seriously enough. Richard learned quickly and easily. While his classmates struggled with their lessons, he kept himself busy by inventing complicated multiplication problems and writing rhymed verses.

At home he tended his rock collection. He also collected stamps and coins from which he learned the geography of the numerous small German states and of the great world beyond.

These happy times in Karlsruhe ended in 1883 when Max Willstätter, a restless man unhappy in the local textile business, decided to seek his fortune in America. Since both parents wanted their sons to have a German education, his young family stayed behind.

To be near her own family, Frau Willstätter moved with her sons to the stern gray city of Nuremburg in Bavaria.

No trees grew along Nuremburg's stony streets, Richard saw at once. Classes at the Latin school were large and the assignments were hard. Among the pupils, prejudice against Jews was strong. So, too, were mockery of the boy's Karlsruhe accent and curiosity about his absent father.

The family soon decided that Richard was not clever at Latin. As a result, for secondary school, he was sent not to the classical and prestigious Gymnasium but to the Realgymnasium. Years later he was taunted for that choice.

In fact, he was grateful for the Realgymnasium. In the school courtyard stood a splendid old elm which he would remember half a century later. Green living things would always please him.

At the Realgymnasium also he found kind and gifted instructors. The once light-hearted boy resolved not to disappoint those fine teachers. He would not be "quite good." He would be "very good." He succeeded so well that on graduation he was recommended for a place in the Royal

Maximilianeum for outstanding Bavarian students. His application was denied. The applicant was a Jew.

Willstätter was not dismayed. He had long ago decided on his life's work. He was good at a wide range of subjects but he thought that he had not a truly great natural talent. He was determined to make a contribution to the world, and to do that he must deliberately concentrate on a single field. When he was only twelve he had chosen chemistry.

His parents did not approve. They wanted him to accept a partnership with an uncle who was a successful businessman. Willstätter turned his back on the offer.

In 1890 he enrolled in the Institute of Technology at the University of Munich. He studied in the University library even on Sundays when the doors were locked. To escape the locked building he managed to climb out a cellar window, tossing his borrowed books out the window before him.

But life was not all book learning. He went to concerts, plays and operas when he had enough money to buy tickets. He drank beer and discussed the problems of the world with friends. His botany class took him on exciting plant collecting trips in the countryside. Geology trips took him high into the Alps.

One organic chemistry lab was an especially exciting challenge. He competed with a fellow student in performing dangerous experiments. The two young men suffered only a few explosions and no injuries but Richard quickly decided that this particular game was senseless. A researcher could improve only by sensible repetition, not by narrow escape from disaster. During vacations he rented a private laboratory where he repeated the hazardous experiments more carefully.

Soon he was accepted as a graduate student to work with Alfred Einhorn who had synthesized anesthetics. Dentists and their patients can still thank Einhorn for novocain. The work in which Willstätter joined was the study of cocaine and similar substances. He would always be fascinated by medical problems.

When he was only twenty-two, he received his Ph.D. His parents and even Professor Einhorn advised him to be practical , to go into industry. During the seventy years since Justus von Liebig had founded his school at Giessen, organic chemistry had laid the foundation for Germany's great manufactures of fertilizer, dyes and drugs. The door to wealth opened that way.

But Richard Willstätter was not interested in manufacturing, using other men's findings. He wanted to explore the unknown.

The next years were not easy. As a young instructor in an authoritarian university, Willstätter was assigned to laboratory space and equipment with teenage students who had neither his experience nor his passion. Rigid rules governed the laboratory. Gas and water might be turned off in the middle of an experiment, and a beginner always needed to be sure he did not offend older professors by invading their fields of research.

None of these difficulties dampened Willstätter's joy in experimentation and his even greater joy in discovery. Nor did they prevent other adventures. He took his first trip to America on the aged Australian steamer, *The Salier*. He visited Boston, New York, Niagara Falls. *The Salier* would soon go down at sea with the loss of all hands, but before that disaster the creaking vessel brought Willstätter safely back to Germany and to his career.

After five years as an instructor, he became a lecturer. He was now head of the organic chemistry department at the University of Munich with a chance to control his own laboratory— and with a salary, his first!

Life offered a fresh treasure. In 1903 horseback riding

near Wiesbaden, he met a friendly Heidelberg professor who invited him to dinner. At the Leser house he met and fell in love with the professor's beautiful and intelligent daughter, Sophie. Etiquette did not allow young couples to be alone together. On their long walks, a breathless but dutiful Professor Leser struggled to keep up with his daughter and her suitor.

Within a few weeks Willstätter managed to propose. In August of 1903 he and Sophie were married. A son, Ludwig, was born the next year and later a daughter, Margarete.

Willstätter accepted a position as professor of chemistry at the Federal Institute of Technology in Zurich. In Switzerland the young couple settled into a country home with a view of lake and mountains and a meadow where Ludwig and Margarete could play. The children were to learn not from a confusion of toys but from trees and flowers and animals.

In 1908 the brief family idyll ended. The young wife died of a ruptured appendix. Hospital rules prevented the night-time operation which could have saved her life.

Willstätter would never remarry. He turned to the care of his children and to his work. He set about investigating the mysteries of chlorophyll.

Chlorophyll, the pigment which gives trees and plants their lovely and varying shades of green, contributes far more than beauty to the world. As Priestley had partially understood and von Liebig had pointed out, if it were not for chlorophyll life on earth would come to an end within one human generation. It is photosynthesis, the action of sunlight upon chlorophyll, which builds organic compounds from carbon dioxide and water. These compounds in turn become sources of energy and the building blocks of plant growth. In the end, they are the sources of animal growth as well, since animals eat plants.

In addition, the chemical reactions involved in photosynthesis release into the air free oxygen which animals and humans need to breathe.

Chlorophyll is the only pigment contained in plants which can cause these life-giving reactions. Some other pigments such as the carotenoids, so bright in carrots and yellow flowers, can be bound up in chloroplasts which contain chlorophyll. These pigments give up their energy to chlorophyll and do not, on their own, cause chemical reactions.

In the early nineteen hundreds, chlorophyll was little understood. Scientists did not even know whether chlorophyll was a single substance. It might differ from plant to plant. If each plant had its own kind of chlorophyll, knowledge about reactions in an oak would not apply to reactions in pine or rose. No one would ever be able to understand the process.

Willstätter began his studies analyzing large quantities of powdered nettles. The prickly, stinging nettle, enemy of hikers and gardeners, was the scientist's good friend. It was cheap, plentiful and uncommonly rich in chlorophyll. In time, with delicate and original experimental techniques, Willstätter obtained "blue-black crystals that shone marvelously like a thousand little jewels" — crystals of pure chlorophyll.

After nettles, Willstätter brought other plants into his laboratory, red seaweed from the English coast, green seaweed from Naples, plants sown in his own garden, in all some two hundred different species.

His study answered the great question. Chlorophyll occurs in slight variations but structurally it is the same substance in sunflower or waterlily, beech or fir. The biochemical process of photosynthesis is universal.

Graduate students were drawn to Zurich and this

research from many countries. With them, especially with Arthur Stoll, who was to be his long-time collaborator, Willstätter studied a wide range of pigments. Always he was in love with the beauty of growing things although he knew, too, the practical use of his work for the drug and dye industries.

Although life in Switzerland was productive, Willstätter remained at heart a German. After seven fruitful years in Zurich he had the chance to become a member of the new Kaiser Wilhelm Institute built on royal lands at Dahlem-Berlin. He accepted eagerly, though he refused to be a director since he did not want to be burdened with routine tasks. He was instead offered complete independence.

Opening yet another new field of organic research, he turned to anthocyanids. Anthocyanids are pigments which cause blue, mauve, purple and violet colors in plants and flowers. Willstätter planted a garden to provide himself with flowers and was especially proud of his red dahlias and roses. Anyone could have done good work with such material, he thought.

But the free happy life at Dahlem did not last. Ten year old Ludwig Willstätter died, his sickness diagnosed too late by his physician.

The Willstätter villa stood in a huge open field where the wind blew fiercely. It was 1914 and the winds of war began to blow more fiercely still.

Many Germans believed that World War I was forced upon them. Willstätter shared that belief. Unable to enlist in the army because of a long ago mountain climbing accident, he offered his services as a scientist. So did many others. His great friend, Fritz Haber, became head of the chemical warfare program. Haber was able to persuade himself that chemical warfare was more humane than guns and tanks.

Willstätter himself, in a short time, developed a remarkably effective gas mask. In spite of his patriotism he was glad that his invention protected rather than destroyed human beings.

In 1915 he was awarded the Nobel Prize in Chemistry for his "researches on plant pigments, especially chlorophyll," but the war prevented any ceremonies or time for rejoicing. The great battles of the Western front were raging. In 1916 the flowers in Willstätter's garden were being carried to patients in Berlin hospitals. His work at Dahlem was ended. Fate led him back to Munich.

Once an obscure student there, he accepted the professorship of chemistry formerly held by Justus von Liebig. It was an honor which moved him but it did not make his life easy. Germany went down to defeat in World War I and German scientists had little money to fund their work. To meet the Allies' demand for fifty tons of gold for war reparations, Fritz Haber set up a giant project for extracting gold from sea water. Sea water turned out to contain far less gold than had once been estimated and Haber's project failed miserably. By 1923, German inflation was so great that Munich beggars asked for billions of paper marks and could not count their take!

Despite all the difficulties of obtaining apparatus, even of providing food for his impoverished young graduate students, Willstätter turned to another new field of research. His friends scolded him. Surely the splendid work on pigments should begin again but "the chemistry of tomorrow is more tempting than the harvesting of a mature crop," Willstätter replied. His beautiful Dahlem dahlias and roses were dead.

More tempting than filling in the gaps which his

previous research had left was the chance to attack new problems. This would both satisfy him and challenge his students with life-long tasks.

Helped by a succession of these students, Willstätter turned to a subject about which he — along with almost everybody else — was ignorant. He chose the study of enzymes.

The behavior of enzymes offers one of the most important of all keys to the secrets of living cells. Enzymes are the catalyst of those cells. They initiate and regulate the chemical reactions which determine the characteristics of organisms. Enzymes themselves remain unchanged.

The enzyme molecule is usually very large. Each can activate other, much smaller molecules, and do so again and again, in some cases, more than one million times per minute.

Enzymes are also highly individual. They are "specific" in their behavior. A particular enzyme can initiate only one kind of reaction.

In the process of animal digestion, for instance, one kind of enzyme is discharged from cells in the mouth and breaks down starches, such as bread and pasta, into simpler substances, more directly useful to the animal body. Another enzyme, secreted in the cells of the stomach, breaks down meat and other proteins.

Some enzymes, not discharged but secreted within living cells, direct the process of metabolism. Some cause the release of energy for immediate use in walking, running, jumping or any of the unnumbered activities of animals and humans.

Willstätter, without today's knowledge, could not dream of charting the structure or synthesizing an enzyme. His goals were more basic.

He determined and isolated enzymes. He investigated

the separation of enzymes from cells. He studied the increase of an enzymic concentration and the specificity of certain enzymes.

There remained unfortunately one problem far more cruel and intractable than the mysteries of science.

Once, a colleague had noticed the picture of Justus von Liebig hanging on Willstätter's office wall.

"Did you know that I am the grandson of von Liebig?" the visitor had demanded.

"We would all wish to be grandsons of von Liebig," Willstätter had replied.

But though he was heir to the science and the position of the great organic chemist, Richard Willstätter was not his grandson in blood. He was the grandson of Jewish rabbis and would always remain loyal to their religion. This he must do, even though he himself did not obey the ancient laws of Judaism which he thought should change with the growth of modern knowledge.

In many times and places, Jews had converted to Christianity to protect themselves against persecution or to further their careers. Fritz Haber had made such a decision. Willstätter could not take that path. For him to become a convert for material gain was immoral.

In time, remaining a part of a university which discriminated against Jews became immoral, too.

As a child he had met with anti-semitism. Over the years he had listened to slurs against his people. He himself, honored abroad, had never been invited to address a full plenary session of the German Chemical Society. All about him he had seen German universities bowing to the growth of anti-semitism.

In 1924, the University of Munich refused to appoint a highly-qualified Jewish scholar, choosing, instead, a much less able man.

In protest, Richard Willstätter resigned his position as professor of chemistry and head of the Chemical Institute. He left forever his beloved laboratory with his precious experimental equipment. Colleagues sent letters of regret. One fellow scientist even called his act "the self-destruction of a great genius." Gradually friends and students dropped away. One day he noticed that his name had disappeared from the university faculty list.

Some of his newly-idle hours he filled with a new adventure. He had long loved beauty in nature — mountains, trees and flowers. Now he sought out beautiful paintings. He was especially attracted to the landscapes of Munich artists. Though he was not rich, he managed to build his collection, purchasing in both Germany and France.

Always he liked pictures painted in the open air by artists uninterested in fame or fortune. "Simple pure souls" he called them.

The true scientist and the artist are not as far apart as people suppose, he said. "We belong together." In old age "we are unspent and unfinished."

Indeed, despite the drastic change in his fortunes, Willstätter's life in science was not yet ended.

As long as Hitler's laws allowed, he continued to consult with German industrial companies although he refused to accept positions with them. At the university, his former student and loyal assistant, Margarete Rohdewald continued joint research on enzymes with him.

Rohdewald worked daily at her laboratory. Each evening she telephoned to report her experimental results. Willstätter worked with the data, making suggestions and plans for future experiments. The resulting papers, products of "Jewish science," could no longer be published in Germany. Even in the United States, papers forty to sixty pages long, written in the German language, were not likely to be best sellers. Yet Willstätter believed his studies in enzymes to be an important part of his life's work.

Scientists in France, Spain, England and the United States remembered him with honors and invitations to lecture. In 1933 he went to Chicago to accept the Willard Gibbs Medal, given in honor of the most notable American theoretical chemist. He was invited to stay on in the United States as a distinguished professor. Other such invitations came from England.

He refused the offers and returned to Munich. The boy whose parents long ago had been separated for seventeen years because they wanted their sons to have a German education, remained German at heart. Germany was his homeland. German culture was his treasure —its literature, art, music, its century of brilliant science.

Perhaps he secretly persuaded himself that the Nazi madness would end. Or perhaps he tried to believe that an aging Nobel Prize winner, whose ancestors had lived so long on German soil, who had himself contributed so much to German science and industry, would be left alone in his small villa with his paintings, his books and his rose garden. Or perhaps, despite all the warnings of disaster, he simply could not face leaving a familiar and well-loved place.

He would stay in Munich as long as possible.

No one else would be harmed by his staying. His wife was here only in vivid memory. His parents were dead. His brother, a business man, had long since emigrated to the United States, fathered a family and died there. His daughter was safe with her physician husband and her children in America.

Yet the terrible warning bells were ringing. In 1933, Adolph Hitler came to power. In 1937, Reichminister Goebbels declared Jews to be "the enemy of the world, the destroyer of civilizations...the formative demon of mankind's destruction."

One November morning in 1938, the final warning came. Margarete Rohdewald telephoned to say that student members of the "National Socialist Automobile Corps" were being asked to pick up Jews for deportation to the death camp at Dachau.

In the afternoon, officers of the Secret State Police appeared at Willstätter's door with orders to take him away.

Willstätter was hidden in the garden among his freezing rose bushes. Inside the villa, Elise Schnauffer, his long-time housekeeper, boldly confronted the SS men. She denied that her master was at home and at her own imperious pace showed them through the house, closet by closet, bed by bed.

In time, the SS men went away without a prisoner. Willstätter awaited their return in his chilled study for three mornings but they did not come back. Perhaps, after all, they meant to give the famous old man a chance to escape.

Willstätter himself saw that he no longer had a choice. He went to the authorities, gave up his passport and announced that he meant to move to Switzerland.

But had he waited too long?

November passed without official permission to emigrate. December passed. January. February. Winter months had never seemed so long.

Willstätter spend fruitless days in government halls trying to get news of what he was required to submit. Payment of half of all he owned as an emigration tax. Payment of the Jewish tax of one-fifth. Listing of every item he meant to take with him even to nail file and toothpaste. The will of his brother who had died in America and might have left him money.

At the end of January his villa was seized. At last he panicked. On a cold and rainy day he took a train to a city on the shores of Lake Constance which lies on the border between Germany and Switzerland. Wet and tired he tramped the windy streets looking for shelter. Every inn displayed the sign "Jews are strictly forbidden."

In despair he let the wind blow him to the shore of the lake. There he discovered an empty row boat. Impulsively, he leapt into it. He had no baggage, no passport, but he would gamble on rowing across the water to Switzerland.

He lost the gamble. SS men found him and took him to the local prison for hours of questioning. Who was he? What had he meant to do?

In that darkest midnight, fortune changed. The high SS officer who led this questioning detained but did not arrest his captive. As soon as his story was confirmed, Willstätter was freed to return to Munich.

Twelve days later he received his passport and the Swiss visa which his long-time friend Arthur Stoll had managed to get for him. In March, with a few possessions including several of his prized paintings, he legally crossed the border into Switzerland.

With Arthur Stoll's help, he was soon settled in southern Switzerland at the villa L'Eremitaggio. His new home stood on a hillside with a lovely terraced garden of semi-tropical fruit. A great camphor tree stood outside his bedroom window. As always, green growing things comforted him.

His researches into the secrets of enzymes had not cleared away all the mysteries he had hoped to solve. It would not be until 1967 that, with new research tools, American biochemists would report the first exact three-dimensional structure of an enzyme. In 1969, the first enzyme would be synthesized in a laboratory.

But Willstätter was still determined to make his contribution. At L'Eremitaggio he wrote his last paper, "The

Enzyme Systems of Sugar Metabolism," published in the journal "Enzymology."

From his refuge he learned of the terrible events taking place in Europe. World War II was beginning. Hitler, he thought, had escaped punishment for his evil deeds inside Germany. Now the wide world must punish him but with such tragedy for so many people.

Willstätter was able to obtain the release of his brother-in-law from a Nazi detention camp in France. Otherwise, he was powerless to influence events or help his friends.

In 1940, his strength was gone. He died in August, just short of his seventieth birthday.

During his life he had received many awards including not only the Nobel Prize but the Willard Gibbs Medal, the Davey Medal, the Farraday Lecture, honorary degrees at Oxford University and the Universities of Manchester and Paris. Yet he had never cared greatly about honors or ceremony. He asked for simple last rites. His ashes were carried to the Lugano Cemetery, accompanied by a few friends and neighbors. Arthur Stoll gave the final, brief tribute.

War and racial prejudice had slashed cruelly across Willstätter's life and career. But he had not lost his courage, Arthur Stoll said. "He let us glimpse the wonder of Creation."

Chapter X

Dorothy Crowfoot Hodgkin

Gentle Genius

In 1927, Sir Arthur Eddington said that more was known about the interior of stars than about the interior of tables. The great British astronomer could not guess that a slim, seventeen-year-old English girl, not yet out of high school, would within ten years be exploring the interior of earthly substances far more mysterious than tables.

Dorothy Crowfoot had been born in Cairo, Egypt, in 1910. She saw the Sphinx and the pyramids of Giza before she saw London Bridge.

An ancient and fascinating land of vast deserts and immense archaeological treasures, Egypt was a protectorate of Great Britain and would not become independent until 1922. Dorothy's father, John Winter Crowfoot, an Oxford-trained classical scholar and archaeologist, was an inspector in the Egyptian Ministry of Education. Her mother, Molly, was a "naturally learned" lady, so her daughter later reported. Molly helped her husband in his archaeological digs, studied botany, drew the flowers of Sudan and became an expert on ancient Coptic textiles. When she had the chance, she was a lively and imaginative tutor to her four daughters.

Molly did not always have that chance. War and the traditions of the British Empire often kept the Crowfoot family apart. Dorothy was four years old when World War I began. She and her younger sisters were left in safety in England, watched over by a nanny and a nearby grandmother. The parents returned to their duties in Egypt. Germans submarines made the seas between them so dangerous that the family was not reunited until war's end.

By now Dorothy was a quiet, self-reliant eight-year-old with soft blond hair and great blue eyes. The years without her mother and father had taught her independence and a strong sense of responsibility for her younger sisters. She would always love and protect children.

With the coming of peace, the Crowfoot family settled near relatives in the village of Geldeston. Molly spent half of each year with her daughters, half with her husband in Egypt and the Sudan. John Crowfoot spent three months annually in England. It was not an unusual pattern for families with fathers stationed in distant parts of the British Empire. That Empire still stood firm in the 1920's.

Dorothy was sent to a succession of small private schools with no clear plan for her education. Perhaps her "naturally learned" mother believed that a Crowfoot would find her own way, as indeed she did. When she was ten she met her first chemistry text book. The book began by describing how to grow copper sulfate and alum crystals. These "flowers of the mineral kingdom" fascinated the little girl. She repeated the school experiments at home.

Chemistry had been a popular hobby for English women of leisure during the early part of the nineteenth century. Women had published their own chemical magazines and eagerly attended lectures.

Such enthusiasm had frightened some male scientists who changed their lectures in order not to shock the ladies or over-tax delicate brains. Such feminine enthusiasm had delighted Joseph Priestley and other members of his Birmingham Lunar Society who believed in higher education for women.

By a curious twist of fate, in the early twentieth century

increasing opportunities gradually turned talented women students away from science. The study of Greek, Latin and literature was far more prestigious.

For her part, young Dorothy was happy to be given special permission to study chemistry with the boys.

Her school life was busy. Molly Crowfoot had lost four brothers in the Great War and was an ardent campaigner for world peace. She took her eldest daughter to a meeting of the League of Nations in Geneva, Switzerland, beginning Dorothy's own life-long devotion to the cause of world peace.

After school hours, Dorothy volunteered for peace campaigns. She joined the Girl Guides who, she later said, taught her the value of international cooperation. When mock elections were held at her school, her mother suggested that she represent the Labour Party which had no candidate. She received only six votes but her interest in the lives of working people was awakened.

At thirteen, she, with a sister, went out to Khartoum in the Sudan where her father was now Director of Education. There she had her second important encounter with chemistry. Her father's friend, A.F. Joseph, a soil chemist, entertained the young visitors by showing them how to pan for gold, finding tiny nuggets in a pile of sand. Dorothy went prospecting in the stream in her family's yard. She did not find gold but she did find a shiny black substance which intrigued her. Joseph helped her identify the mineral ilmenite. He was so impressed with her eagerness that he gave her a real surveyor's box with blowpipe, minerals and reagents, substances which cause chemical reactions.

Dorothy took her new treasure back to England and set up her own laboratory at home.

On her sixteenth birthday, her mother gave her a book called *Concerning the Nature of Things*. The author was

Nobel Prize winner William Henry Bragg. With his twenty-two-year-old son Lawrence, youngest Nobelist ever, Bragg had made an epochal advance—a way to use the x-rays discovered by Wilhelm Roentgen to determine the arrangement of atoms in a crystal. "The discovery of x-rays has increased the keenness of our vision over ten-thousand times and we can now 'see' the individual atoms and molecules," Bragg wrote.

It was an astonishing claim, Dorothy thought. And how many crystals there were to be "seen"!

The new process would not prove to be quite as simple as Bragg's cheerful book for young readers seemed to suggest.

In the early twentieth century x-ray diffraction was thought of as a kind of "black art." Traditional chemists, following the patient Berzelius, had determined the structure of solid materials by degradation — meltihg, vaporizing or bringing them into solution. This tedious but important work had revealed properties of many substances. It could not hint at the <u>reason</u> for these properties or predict any useful way of changing them.

Gases, liquids and solids like glass and plastic are called "amorphous." They have no regular interior pattern. Most solids, however , nearly all metals, minerals and alloys, are made up of crystals with characteristic shapes. These crystals are in turn made up of repeated, three-dimensional arrangements of atoms and molecules. Nature is so orderly that only one out of a thousand atoms is likely to be out of place in such a design. Atoms and the spaces between them are, however, so tiny that they cannot be seen under the most powerful microscope using ordinary light.

In 1912, Max von Laue, a young German physicist, discovered that x-rays, four thousand times shorter than light rays, when directed at a crystal of copper sulfate were bent as they passed through the crystal. These bent or "diffracted" rays made a mysterious pattern of small dots on a photographic plate.

The Braggs, father and son, built on this discovery. It was young Lawrence who announced the atomic structure of sodium chloride, common table salt, the first structure ever determined by x-ray. World-wide research with this new tool began.

Though Dorothy was quickly fascinated, much preparation lay ahead for her.

She graduated from school and decided to go to Oxford to "read"—to major in—chemistry. Generous Aunt Dorothy Hood would help her with finances.

But there were serious gaps in her preparation. She had never studied Latin or a second science. What was more, much as she loved chemistry, she was tempted by archaeology.

The six months after high school she spent with her mother and father who were now in Transjordan excavating Byzantine churches. The work was at Basra, Sumeria and Jerash, the old Roman "city of a thousand columns" on the desert's edge. Dorothy's parents found that she was good at drawing the patterns of the ancient mosaic floors. She loved the work but, in the end, chemistry prevailed.

During her months in the Near East she studied Latin and physics on her own. Her mother taught her botany. She returned to England, passed the Oxford entrance examinations and enrolled in Somerville College.

Somerville had been only the second women's college founded at Oxford. The rules governing women's lives were strict. They could not join the debating society or other important student organizations. On campus they were allowed to wear the black gowns prescribed for men but not the mortar boards — only soft and unbecoming black caps.

They could not go into men's rooms for tea or lunch without a chaperon and previous permission from the dean. Living quarters and even meals were drab, quite unlike the accommodations and servants available to men students.

Men were much concerned about the "virility" of their university. They were fearful that in the future their brothers would choose to attend Cambridge rather than Oxford since Cambridge did not have many women students. In response to these fears, Oxford decided to limit the number of coeds. The venerable institution must continue to be a haven for gentlemen's sons with the addition of only a few gentlemen's daughters.

By Dorothy's time, graduates of Somerville College received degrees. It would be another half century before full co-education was granted.

Yet women, even those who resisted, loved the combination of heady freedom and strict regulation which Somerville College offered. The mystery writer Dorothy Sayers, a rebellious Somerville student, wrote of Oxford as an "enchanted town", though she once wore to breakfast what her faculty regarded as "offending bedizement"— nearly shoulder length earrings which modeled green and scarlet parrots in gilt cages!

Dorothy Crowfoot's style was not rebellion. In her long career it would never be. Quiet but unwavering independence was her mode.

As a woman majoring in science, Dorothy was a rare creature. She seems to have been too busy to mind. There was so much to learn. She spent much of her first year getting better acquainted with physics. She was glad, she later said, to have learned little about the subject before she came to college. Being ignorant, she could have the excitement of discovering everything for herself.

Her professors soon recognized her talent. Margery Fry,

principal of Somerville, became her fast friend. One teacher encouraged her to do a chemical analysis of the tesserae, or tiny pieces of the glass mosaics she had drawn and brought back from Transjordan. At vacation time he loaned her his platinum crucible and the key to his office. Her tutor in another course urged her to enter crystallography.

X-ray diffraction, in principle so easy to explain, was not a science for the impatient. Determining the interior structure of a crystal could be compared to determining the shape of a jungle gym by studying its shadow.

Each crystal had to be photographed dozens of times from many different angles. The researcher must then study the intensity of the dots produced by the diffracted x-rays upon the photographic plates. Some dots were small and faint. Others were big and dark. Once the intensities were analyzed, thousands of calculations must be made to determine the crystal's structure.

Though Dorothy became remarkably good at this work, no job awaited her when she "went down" or graduated from Somerville. Luckily A.F. Joseph, her old friend from gold-panning days in the Sudan, rescued her. In a chance encounter on a train, he met a noted chemist who told him that John Bernal, the pioneering crystallographer at Cambridge University, needed an assistant. The pay was small but the opportunity was great. Aunt Dorothy was generous with financial aid once again.

Dorothy spent two years at Cambridge living a young scientist's dream. John Bernal was a hearty, brilliant man with wide-ranging curiosity and a great store of knowledge in many fields. He believed strongly in equal opportunity for women. His new assistant was warmly welcomed to the laboratory luncheons with their shared food and sparkling conversation.

She soon set to work analyzing the many crystals sent to

the Cambridge laboratory. Before long, she was earning a reputation for "clearing Bernal's desk." There was "gold" all over that desk, she said. In 1934, Bernal took a landmark photograph which showed that proteins, vital to the functioning of the human body, could be crystallized and so studied by x-ray diffraction. It would be possible for Dorothy to realize her dream of "seeing" important bio-chemical molecules.

On the day of Bernal's photograph, she learned that the increasing pain in her hands was caused by advanced rheumatoid arthritis for which there was no cure and which would increasingly cripple her. Despite that problem, she had a living to earn. In 1934, she returned to Oxford to complete her Ph.D. degree and to teach chemistry in the women's colleges.

Her faculty life at Oxford in those early years was lonely. As a woman she could not attend the faculty's weekly discussions of current chemical research. Only the student chemical club asked her to speak. Her "ghoulish" laboratory deep in the basement of Oxford University Museum was neighbor to dinosaur bones and dried beetles. The only natural light came from one high window reached by climbing a rickety stair. There was little research equipment.

In Bernal's laboratory Dorothy had been a gentle but brilliant presence with iron determination and a practical turn of mind. She remained so. Boldly, she asked a senior professor to find money for the new apparatus which she needed. Impressed with her careful preparation, the professor persuaded a British company to finance the purchase of cameras and x-ray tubes. Gradually she received other small grants.

With the new equipment and the help of one graduate student she set about studying the sterol crystals, especially cholesterol, essential to so many living organisms. Recent research had proved cholesterol to be made up of carbon, hydrogen and oxygen. These elements were common enough, but how were the individual atoms arranged in a three-dimensional shape?

Dorothy, as she would always do, had chosen a study just beyond the range of the "possible." Thousands of calculations led, at last, to a solution and a joyous jig about her laboratory. She had "seen" the structure of cholesterol!

By now she was developing delicate, new techniques. She became expert at interpreting electron density charts. Often, having an incomplete picture of a molecule, she could create a second crystal exactly like the first except for the addition of a single different heavy atom. A comparison of the x-ray diffraction patterns of the two samples helped her to "see" the pattern of the first. To appreciate the delicacy of the work one can remember that on an average ten million atoms touching each other form a line one millimeter in length.

The work went on. Dorothy proceeded to grow insulin crystals, a project of great medical importance.

Insulin is the hormone necessary for sugar metabolism in the body. Human beings normally produce their own insulin. A failure to produce the hormone causes diabetes. Despite the medical importance of insulin, even Dorothy was forced to admit that the crystal was far too large to study by any methods yet devised. She put away this project but she would not forget it.

In 1937 she received her Ph.D. degree. In that same year, the young woman who had signed her first scientific papers as Dorothy Crowfoot became Dorothy Hodgkin. Her husband, Thomas Hodgkin, was a cousin of her good friend Margery Fry. He was a member of a Quaker family which had for generations produced noted scientists and historians. He was merry and talkative, a lover of good food, good wine and good friendships. He was also a champion of the underdog and had recently resigned a government post in Palestine because of sympathy for the Arabs who were rebelling against British rule there.

Like Dorothy's mentor, John Bernal, Thomas had joined the Communist Party in the belief that a Marxist society would be humane and rational, benefitting common people. Dorothy did not follow her husband into the Party but she shared many of his concerns. For nearly ten years Thomas organized and taught classes for the unemployed in the North of England. On weekends, the couple traveled to be together since Dorothy continued her work at Oxford. Thomas was convinced that "Dossie" was more creative than he and was resolved to see that she had the chance to use her gifts.

During these years, the Hodgkins had three children. After Thomas became Director of Extramural Studies at Oxford, the family was able to live together. Eventually they moved into a big, cluttered house to which they welcomed one of Dorothy's sisters, her four children, servants and a continuing stream of guests. It was no hermit life.

In the meantime, World War II had broken out. Penicillin, recently discovered by Alexander Fleming and his co-workers, could save the lives of many of the sick and wounded which that war was sure to bring. Unfortunately, the new antibiotic, derived from the penicillium mold, could not be produced in large quantities by natural means. A way to produce it synthetically was desperately needed.

Researchers in the United States and England set to work. At Oxford, Dorothy Hodgkin with one assistant began to study the penicillin molecule as soon as useful specimen were available.

Two elderly refugees from the Blitz and a loving grandmother helped to care for the Hodgkin children.

Working in her laboratory seemed to Hodgkin herself "the natural thing to do."

Success would not prove easy. Penicillin turned out to be extraordinarily hard to analyze. Nobody had guessed that its crystals come not in one shape but in different shapes. Nobody knew that a slight change in conditions changes the way the molecules act within the crystal. And there was the complication of the single sulfur atom within the molecule.

Hodgkin's early reports astonished her colleagues. One famous chemist announced that he would retire from his university position and grow mushrooms if Hodgkin proved to be right about penicillin. She was proved right, the doubter did not retire and lengthy calculations went on. After four years of research Hodgkin's laboratory produced the first accurate model of a penicillin crystal. Even with its structure understood, penicillin proved hard to synthesize. Valuable semi-synthetic penicillins were manufactured following Hodgkin's model.

She had become by now an acknowledged mistress of crystallography. Crystallography itself, though still thought of as a "black art" by some fearful organic chemists, was generally recognized as a science with valuable applications.

Hodgkin's life was growing increasingly exciting and complicated. She helped to found the International Union of Crystallographers. At the age of thirty-seven, she was elected to the Royal Society, that venerable institution of researchers founded in the seventeenth century as the "invisible college." She was the third woman member in the Society's long history.

Oxford gave Hodgkin a university appointment with a salary which at last helped to balance the family budget. Her once "ghoulish" laboratory was gradually enlarged. Eager graduate students, including ambitious young women, came to study with her. She welcomed and mothered all, helping the young women find jobs in a male-dominated scientific world.

Always her research group was small, no more than ten. She chose it that way. In wistful moments, she might envy the flood of new crystal studies which began to come from large laboratories around the world. She herself did not want to direct research at a distance from her assistants. One visitor to her group wrote that she was "their gentle lady boss who can out-think and out-guess them on any score." Contrary to the usual scientific practice, when papers were published, the names of all those who had a part in the research were listed alphabetically as authors.

Thomas Hodgkin's life was changing, too. Descended from a long line of historians, he turned to African history, pointing out that the Dark Continent had a vibrant past. He was especially attracted to the emerging government of Kwame Nkrumah of Ghana. Ghana was the first of Africa's former colonial Black nations to become independent. At Legon, its university had one of the loveliest African campuses. White stucco buildings with red tile roofs stood among bright green lawns and gardens.

Thomas was appointed Director of African Studies at Legon. For three years his wife flew out regularly to visit him. Interested and welcomed by people wherever she went, she enjoyed the handsome Ghanian people.

None of the excitements of the passing years, however, kept her from devotion to her own laboratory work. One day a drug company chemist, knowing of her work with penicillin, brought her some tiny, deep red crystals of Vitamin B_{12}. Yet another major study of her career began.

Vitamin B_{12} is the only cure for the otherwise fatal disease of pernicious anemia. As with penicillin, drug companies could not hope to manufacture the life-saving vitamin in quantity until they knew its structure.

The B_{12} molecule is larger than the penicillin molecule and still more complicated. Most crystallographers thought that its puzzles could not be solved by existing techniques.

For six years Hodgkin and her group studied Vitamin B_{12}. They took twenty-five hundred x-ray photographs. Luckily, help came from a visiting American who had pioneered a high speed electronic computer for crystallography. In a pre-fax, pre-e-mail world, they collaborated by mail and cables, with Hodgkin always confident that in the end she would get the answer she sought.

Some people believed she was too confident but once again she was right. Eight years after the work began, she announced the structure of B_{12} , a molecule composed of sixty-three atoms of carbon, eighty-eight of hydrogen, fourteen of oxygen and one each of phosphorous and cobalt. Small wonder the search had been long!

In 1964, Hodgkin was visiting her husband in Africa when the news arrived that she had been awarded the Nobel Prize in Chemistry for her work on penicillin and B_{12} . At home in England, London's "Daily Mail" announced "Nobel Prize for British Wife." Less chauvinist, the local African newspaper claimed "Ghana's First Nobel." The university staged lively celebrations with dancing under the stars. A dressmaker in the capital city of Accra created a dress of gold China silk for the awardee to wear to the ceremony in Stockholm.

Family and friends came to Sweden from far-flung places around the world. Sister Diane could not attend since she heard the news at a station near the North Pole and telegraphed her husband at another station near the South Pole. Hodgkin's Nobel address was matter-of-factly entitled "The X-ray Analysis of Complicated Matter."

Other awards and honorary degrees were crowding upon her. In 1965 she became the second woman to be awarded the British Order of Merit. The first woman awardee had been the famous nurse Florence Nightingale nearly sixty years earlier. At a banquet of celebration, the artist Henry Moore sketched the arthritis-crippled hands with which Hodgkin had performed her delicate work.

There still remained the pesky problem of insulin with its seven hundred and seventy-seven atoms. Sophisticated computers had now made that analysis possible, she decided. With the computers as aid, Hodgkin and her group studied the density of tens of thousands of dots on x-ray photographs. In 1969, she was able to announce that the mystery of insulin's crystal structure was solved. It was her final notable scientific achievement. She left her Oxford laboratory in 1977.

The end of active research was not the end of other projects. In retirement she said that her hobbies were "archaeology, walking and children." She delighted in her grown children, her grandchildren and great-grandchildren. Broader interests claimed her also.

She had kept alive, life-long, the passion for world peace and international cooperation instilled in her by her mother. From the beginning, her International Union of Crystallographers had insisted that membership be open to scientists of all countries, both the defeated and the victorious in World War II, both capitalists and communists. Union meetings were not held in a country which denied entry to citizens of any land.

Hodgkin herself traveled widely. The progressive crippling of her hands and feet did not stop her, as it had never kept her from handling delicate crystals.

Everywhere people talked freely to her. She visited the countries of Eastern and Western Europe, Russia, Africa, China, Vietnam, the United States—although she was not always granted an American visa. She had carefully kept politics out of her laboratory and was little interested in political theory, only in ordinary people and their lives. The U.S. government, however, wary and fearful during the Cold War, was distrustful of her membership in "Science for Peace," an organization which included some communists. They refused to let her enter the country. Later, when she was old and crippled, her passport was approved.

In 1975, Hodgkin became president of the Pugwash Conferences on Science and World Affairs. The organization campaigned for world peace and disarmament. "If some — and preferably all — of the million dollars spent every minute on arms were turned to the abolition of poverty in the world, many causes of conflict would vanish," she wrote. The Pugwash president could well have been a figure-head, lending only the prestige of her name. But the cause of peace was too important to her. Hodgkin chose to be active and hard-working.

Thomas Hodgkin, after his own venturesome life, died in 1982. Hodgkin herself lived on in a stone cottage in the Cotswold region. Wheel-chair bound, she died of a stroke on July 29, 1994.

Many modern feminists have hoped that career women would bring humane and caring qualities to the professional world. With her many scientific accomplishments, Dorothy Crowfoot Hodgkin, the gentle genius, was one who fulfilled that feminist dream.

Chapter XI
Linus Pauling
Asset to the Human Race

In a mathematics course the only passing grade should be 100%, Linus Pauling declared.

Not everybody would agree. Not everybody, after all, has learned to count to 100 in Chinese on an abacus at the age of two. But Linus Pauling offered good reasons for demanding perfection. That was one of the things he liked about mathematics. You could be perfect.

But if you got only 70% in your first math class, in your second class you would probably understand 70% of the first 70%— which is 49% of what you need to know. Very soon you would understand so little that you would give up altogether. A great pity!

No one — except perhaps the Chinese merchant with the abacus who had taught the toddler — could have predicted Pauling's own gift for mathematics. Anyone might have predicted his determination and his thirst for the new and undiscovered.

Westerners are the real Americans, Pauling once said. Members of his own Westering family had followed the Oregon Trail to carve out new lives for themselves in the Oregon territory. His great-great grandfather, so the boy was told, had made the trek in 1844 at the age of eighty-three. His grandfather, Linus Darling, had worked his way across the continent as a runaway "bound boy."

Linus' own father, Herman, was the son of a German-speaking iron-monger who had adventured to

California and, finding no fortune there, gone north to Oregon.

Herman Pauling was an intense young man with dreams of glory. A traveling drug salesman with a grammar school education, he was resolved that his wife and children would one day live in luxury. He was also resolved that each one of his children would be "an asset to the human race."

Linus, the oldest of the three children, was born on February 28, 1901, in Portland, Oregon. When he was four years old, the family moved to Condon where Mrs. Pauling had lived as a girl. There Herman Pauling took charge of the local drug store which stocked, among other items, "Pauling's Pink Pills for Pale People" and "Dr. Pfunder's Oregon Blood Purifier." The Purifier was billed as "an almost certain cure" for diseases ranging from liver trouble to dyspepsia and pimples.

Despite the patent medicines on his shelves, Herman Pauling was not a quack. He had studied *The Pharmacopoeia of the United States* and knew how to mix drugs. He was much interested in public health and may have offered the best medical advice available to his community.

That community, Condon, was a frontier settlement on the high, dry and treeless plateau east of the Cascade Mountains. Some five hundred people lived there. Cowboys tramped the dusty main street. Indians camped on the outskirts of town. The boy Linus was free to get into mischief with his cousins and the Indian boys, wander into the drug store to watch his father mix strange potions, roam out to the neighboring wheat fields and listen to the field hands spin tall tales, stay outdoors till dark.

School lessons were easy. Linus developed such a love of reading that his proud father wrote to the "Oregonian", the state's biggest newspaper, asking what books to choose for

172

his precocious son. Respondents were please not to suggest the Bible or Charles Darwin. His son was already acquainted with them.

All in all, life in Condon was good for a boy. It did not fulfill the dreams of his parents.

When Linus was nine years old, the family moved back to Portland. With high hopes, Herman set up a new drug store complete with glittering soda fountain. A few months later, he died.

For Belle Pauling, the sudden death was disastrous. She bravely converted the family home into a boarding house, but she was not strong physically and she knew nothing about business. She had loved her husband very much. She was not so close to her children. Her son especially was a mystery to her and would remain so.

He did not seem to want to make friends in the city. Instead he continued to love books and got the most unsettling ideas from them. He persuaded a druggist friend of the family to give him some potassium cyanide, a poison. This chemical he poured into one of his mother's Mason jars under fifty grams of plaster of Paris and so created a killing jar for the insects which he enthusiastically collected. He also collected rocks and built himself a laboratory in the boarding house basement where he could work with his collections and be alone.

Worse, he left paper-wrapped packets of potassium chlorate and sulfur on trolley car tracks and cheered in triumph at the bang the chemicals made when the trolley wheels passed over them. The authorities came to Belle's boarding house to complain.

It was in the home of his one close friend, Lloyd Jeffress, also very smart and also fatherless, that the thirteen-year-old Linus decided on his future. He watched Lloyd mix bright powders until they bubbled and changed color. More impressively, he saw table sugar blend with two other simple chemicals to become black carbon. He was entranced. In chemistry, things didn't stay the same. In chemistry, things happened. Remarkable things. He would become a chemist.

At Portland's Washington High School, he took the usual liberal arts courses, including four years of Latin. He also took all the science and mathematics which the school offered. Already he had decided to go to college.

He chose Oregon Agricultural College (now Oregon State University). OAC was in Corvallis, only ninety miles from Portland and tuition there was nearly free.

Belle Pauling, frail and poor, disapproved. She had expected that once her son had finished high school he would take a job and help support his mother and sisters. She herself had been so miserable in her one year at boarding school that she could not imagine why anyone would leave home to seek higher education.

Sixteen-year-old Linus refused to change his mind. During his years at OAC, he sent money to his mother and supported himself at a variety of jobs. He chopped wood, mopped floors, cut up beef, worked in a shipyard, delivered milk, inspected highway pavements.

Fortunately the friendly faculty at the "Chem Shack", which housed a growing chemistry department, did not mean to lose their star pupil to manual labor. Pauling was offered jobs within the department.

Like many a young chemist, as a lab assistant he had a near-fatal accident. He burned off a part of the mucous membrane of his mouth. He was not frightened. Rather, he was growing more and more fascinated.

In his general chemistry text book, Pauling found the word "stochastic." "Stochastic" comes from Greek and is the name for a method of research. Using the "stochastic" method, a chemist makes a hypothesis — an informed guess.

Then he carries out experiments to prove or disprove his hypothesis. It is a method which works beautifully for a chemist with imagination. Pauling, richly endowed, believed in imagination. He declared that, in fact, the chemical researcher needs more imagination then most other people do.

But he did not spend all his time at OAC in the laboratory. He joined a fraternity. He enrolled in the student Officer's Training Corps and became a major. He went out, not very successfully, for track. He got interested in public speaking and in his junior year entered an oratorical contest with a paper entitled "Children of the Dawn."

"We are not the flower of civilization," he said. "We are the children of the dawn, witnessing the approach of the day. We bask in the dim prophesies of the rising sun, knowing, even in our own inexperience, that something glorious is to come. For it is from us that greater beings will grow to develop in the light of the sun that shall know no setting."

"Children of the Dawn" did not win first prize. It did express Pauling's strong belief in human progress and in science as the path to the future. It hinted at the individual scientist's duty to contribute to "something glorious."

In the second semester of his senior year, the Boy Professor, tall, curly-haired with intense blue eyes, taught a chemistry course for home economics majors. At the first class meeting he glanced down the roster and called on "Miss Miller." He did not know which of the twenty-five coeds was Miss Miller but he could not possibly mispronounce her name and risk setting the coeds to giggling. "Miss Miller, will you please tell me what you know about baking powder?"

Dark-haired Ava Helen Miller answered his question in detail. She was, he promptly decided, both very pretty and very bright. By commencement time they were engaged to be married.

It was the year 1922. A new world was about to open before the twenty-one-year-old from Oregon.

His OAC professors were not notable research men. They were devoted teachers, recognized talent and urged their students to go on to graduate study. Pauling applied to the California Institute of Technology.

Only a few years before Caltech had been Throop College, a manual training school. Its future even now was uncertain. But it had a brilliant chemistry department chair, and it offered Pauling a generous fellowship with much freedom. He accepted at once.

Regretfully leaving Ava Helen at OAC to continue her own education, he went south to Pasadena. The next year he returned north in a second-hand Model-T Ford to be married.

He and Ava Helen shared a common dream. Linus would earn his Ph.D. and become a famous chemistry professor. Ava Helen would take charge of their children and the practical details of their lives. Ava Helen was an intelligent and modern young woman with a strong social conscience. But her husband was, as she did not doubt, a genius. She would free him to do his work.

By now chemistry was defined as the study of the behavior of molecules. Chemists were beginning to realize that the characteristics of substances and the ways in which they reacted with each other depended on the arrangement of atoms which made up the molecules.

Pauling's first published paper, co-authored with his professor, described the structure of molybdenite. Molybdenite, so the paper reported, is a shiny black mineral made up of six atoms of sulfur, forming an equal-sided prism around one atom of molybdenum. It was the first structure

of its kind which had ever been found. Pauling was elated.
It was wonderful to discover something that no one else had
known before.

The tool he used was the x-ray diffraction apparatus,
which had been recently perfected by the English physicists,
William and Lawrence Bragg, and which Dorothy Hodgkin
would in a few years use to such good effect. His apparatus
directed a beam of x-rays through a fine grating upon a
carefully-prepared crystal sample. The x-rays, deflected by
the atoms within the molecules of the substance, formed a
pattern upon his photographic screen. By "backward
reasoning," he could determine the arrangement of atoms
within the molecule. Each substance displayed its own
particular pattern.

The process, as Hodgkin would discover, was simple to
state but complicated and time-consuming to carry out.
Difficulties were many.

No one who has seen pictures of the mushroom cloud
rising above the New Mexico desert at Alamogordo, where
the first atomic bomb was exploded, can doubt that atoms
and molecules are real and potentially powerful. They are
also unimaginably tiny.

Though such minute particles cannot be studied under
ordinary light, some readily give up their secrets to x-rays.
For a variety of reasons, some substances give up their
secrets reluctantly or not at all.

Pauling himself had worked for a few frustrating months
with poor results. Before long, however, he became a master
of the x-ray diffraction technique. By means of x-ray
diffraction, and the later less time-consuming electron
diffraction, the patterns of some two hundred substances
would over the years be determined in his laboratory.

More than a master of apparatus, Pauling became a
master of theory. Determining molecular structure alone did

not satisfy him. He was tantalized by other unknowns, including the old questions with which Jacob Berzelius a century earlier had struggled. Why and how do certain atoms join to form molecules? How and why do certain elements join with other elements to form compounds?

Why, for instance, does hydrogen combine most often with other elements? Why is carbon a close runner-up, making possible a whole important branch of chemistry, the study of carbon compounds?

Why do the rare gases, such as helium, not combine at all? Why do the "noble metals", silver and gold, hesitate to combine in air or water?

Despite genius and decades of hard work, Berzelius had never answered the basic question. Younger chemists had ruthlessly torn apart his "dualistic" theory but had come up with no better—sometimes worse—answers of their own. Nineteenth century science simply did not have enough knowledge or possess delicate enough tools to ferret out the secret.

At the end of the nineteenth century, physics, chemistry's sister—and sometimes rival—science had come to the rescue. Five years before Linus Pauling had been born, the English physicist J.J. Thomson had proved the existence of the electron. In 1911, Ernest Rutherford had discovered the atomic nucleus.

The electron is a particle inside an atom. It carries a negative electric charge and moves about the nucleus of the atom. The nucleus itself contains particles called neutrons which have no electric charge and particles called protons which have positive electrical charge. Each atom of a particular element has a specific number of electrons matched by an equal number of protons.

Electrons have sometimes been pictured as miniature

planets moving in near-circular orbits about their sun, the atomic nucleus.

The reality is not so simple. Electrons appear to be located in "shells" about a nucleus and do not ordinarily trespass into the space between shells.

Nobody can predict the exact position of one particular electron at a given instant, and some make the jump from level to level. Contrary to the laws of classical physics they never lose their charge and they never collapse into the nucleus.

Clearly, Newtonian mechanics, which works so well on earth and on space stations and perhaps on Mars, does not work inside the atom. New explanations were needed. Quantum physics, quantum mechanics — the concept of light as made up of both waves and packets called quanta — the so-called uncertainty principle and other physical theories still mystify and sometimes mislead non-scientists. For adventurous chemists they flashed a bright light into age-old mysteries. Physical chemistry became an exciting game.

As a physical chemist, Pauling was trained by both American and European professors, as well as by his own voracious reading in the three interlocking disciplines, mathematics, chemistry and the new physics. Always intent on bringing order out of chaos, he determined to draw the three sciences together. He had before him the pioneering work of, among others, the American chemist Irving Langmuir of the General Electric Company, winner of the Nobel Prize, and Gilbert N. Lewis of the University of California at Berkeley.

It was known by now that atoms "want" to become stable. But some do not have the necessary number of electrons. In their drive to become stable, atoms of highly-reactive elements, like hydrogen and carbon, attach themselves to other atoms by means of unpaired electrons. They may share electrons or they may give or receive them. The connections may be strong and difficult to break. They may be weak and easily torn apart. They may vary or "resonate" back and forth. Other factors, too, affect the process.

In developing his explanation, the young Linus Pauling spent hardworking and happy years. Life was good. His family was growing. There would be three sons and a daughter. In 1925 he received his Ph.D. with highest honors from a school that was rapidly becoming a world center for scientific research. In 1926, with Ava Helen he went abroad for the first time to visit European laboratories. In 1927, he became a faculty member of the chemistry department at Caltech.

In 1931, Pauling published his own favorite paper which would win for him the Irving Langmuir Prize for a chemist under thirty. The paper, like the immensely influential book which followed, was called "The Nature of the Chemical Bond." When he went east to deliver the paper in person, the auditorium lights went out as he called for the showing of his slides. He went on calmly and steadily lecturing in an auditorium lit only by the firefly flicker of cigarette tips. It was a performance which his audience would long remember. A year later, Pauling became the youngest person ever elected to the American Academy of Sciences.

Within a few years philosophers were beginning to build systems based on the "new physics", but Pauling was not interested in philosophy. He liked quantum mechanics because it worked in the real world of atoms, molecules and crystals. In 1947, he would publish the widely-popular text book *General Chemistry*, later revised as *College Chemistry*, which brought his views to generations of American students.

But Pauling was restless. For him, the natural world was a thrilling obstacle course always presenting new hurdles.

The structure of many minerals and metals had now been determined in his laboratories. It was valuable work. Understanding structure and bonding of minerals and metals would help chemists create countless new and useful materials. The very strength and hardness of metals like steel depend on the strength of chemical bonds.

But what of plant and animal tissues? What of the proteins, that special group of enzymes without which there could be no living matter? Understanding their structure might lead to the end of much human suffering.

The human body contains many hundreds of different proteins each with its own specific function. Many of these molecules are much larger than those of metals. Thousands of atoms may join to make up a single protein molecule. The atoms form "polypeptide chains" some of which fold into three-dimensional shapes.

For such complicated structures, diffraction pictures are blurry, hard to interpret. Pauling, who often used flamboyant models of molecules in his lectures, began to make paper models for his own research. He even asked himself how he would fold if he were a peptide chain!

Pauling's research was interrupted by life-threatening Bright's disease which he with his doctor's help managed to conquer. Research was interrupted also by World War II.

Pauling did much war work. He was part of a program for designing explosives and rocket propellants. He made invisible inks for sending secret messages. He helped develop a synthetic blood plasma.

In a three-day train trip across the United States, he designed a device for measuring oxygen content of the atmosphere in submarines and airplanes, a device which after the war would help save the lives of incubator babies.

He served on governmental committees and traveled to hospitals around the country, planning future medical research.

When peace came, he was awarded the National Medal of Merit. Other honors crowded in upon him from his own country and abroad, from England, France, India, Japan, and, in time, Russia, with numerous invitations to lecture. Many of the invitations he accepted. The old Greek historian Herodotus had said that scholars should travel and Pauling followed that advice.

He also returned to speculation about the still un-solved structure of proteins, providing the theories which his students and colleagues worked to prove or disprove in the laboratory.

He was especially intrigued by the protein hemoglobin, present in red blood cells. He learned that in sickle-cell anemia, a hereditary disease of people of African origin, blood cells are "sickled" or twisted out of shape when they are carried in the veins of the human body. In the arteries, fortified by the oxygen from freshly-breathed air, they change to their normal shape.

Sickle-cell anemia must be a genetic disease caused by a defect in the hemoglobin molecule, Pauling guessed. Several years' research with a careful co-worker proved him right.

Sickle-cell anemia became the first known molecular disease. Its discovery started a whole new field of research.

But now for the first time in his life Pauling became involved in a world less manageable than the comfortingly reasonable world of molecules. It was the world of politics and social policy.

In 1948, he was sworn in as president-elect of the American Chemical Society. At once he began to seek new funds for scientific research and to champion the right of free speech for scientists and for all Americans. At the time, Senator Joseph McCarthy and the House un-American Activities Committee were investigating citizens for reputed loyalty to Russian communism. Pauling's outspoken attack on the Committee focused their attention upon him. Soon he himself was under investigation and accused of being a Communist.

Twenty-four years of FBI investigations failed to produce any evidence that the charges were true. But for a time they had a sad effect upon Pauling's life. Funding for his research became difficult to obtain. For several years he was refused a U.S. passport and so could not attend international scientific meetings. He was called before investigating committees in California as well as Washington.

Once his eyes were opened to problems in the larger world he was willing to do battle for a range of causes. When he thought of the human suffering and the one hundred million deaths caused by World War II, all wars, except those of direct self-defense, appalled him.

Only a system of international law, he thought, would ever keep nations from fighting each other and using that terrible new weapon, the atomic bomb. He was certain that the United States could not long keep the secret of the bomb, as Russian scientists soon proved. He wanted the U.S. Cabinet to include a Secretary of Peace and the government itself to take the lead in bringing about world peace.

Eloquently he laced his public speeches with such startling lines as "it is the atomic bomb which is responsible for my being here tonight — just as the atomic bomb may be responsible for our all not being here a few years from now."

He asked his listeners to imagine themselves two-hundred-and-fifty-thousand miles tall — moon-tall people. On that vast scale, an atom would be only the size of a billiard ball. Yet the tiny nucleus of the uranium atom, when used in a bomb, could be bombarded with particles called neutrinos setting up a chain reaction of such power that whole cities — whole nations — might be incinerated.

The very testing of atomic bombs and, after 1954, the more powerful hydrogen bombs, even in remote parts of the earth, was extremely dangerous to human beings because of harmful fallout radiation, Pauling argued. Some scientists insisted that he exaggerated the dangers of fallout. He did not swerve. The testing of bombs must stop.

He signed petition after petition supporting pacifist and what he considered progressive views. He did not question other names upon these petitions when the causes appeared right to him. Perhaps he believed that all people who signed the petition were sincere and honorable, what he had called in his long ago college days "children of the dawn."

Meantime the drama of his scientific research must go on. He worked with immunology, trying to determine how the human body protects itself. How do anti-bodies kill off — or sometimes *not* kill off — the invading antigens which carry diseases? Pauling's conclusions were sometimes proved right, sometimes wrong. Always they stimulated further research.

Another challenging problem concerned heredity. As everyone can observe, people receive traits from their parents and pass them on to their children. How does this genetic information travel from generation to generation?

In 1944, it had been proved that molecules of DNA (deoxyribonucleic acid) have the unique ability to transfer genetic information. DNA molecules are the code-bearers in the cells of the human body. They see to it that, for better or for worse, Great-Grandpa's nose, Grandma's bright blue eyes —and in some cases their unwelcome diseases—do not vanish from the genetic storehouse.

What intricate arrangement allows the molecules to do this amazing work?

Today, the DNA structure is compared to a twisted rope ladder— spiraling strands or tubes of amino acids, the building blocks of proteins.

In the early 1950's, a crucial question was not yet answered. How many spirals, or helices, occur within the DNA molecule? What exact shape would allow the genetic code-bearer to function?

There were many more limited questions to ask along the path to the final answer. Pauling asked and answered some of these questions in a series of brilliant papers. Others also were busy. Two young Englishmen, Francis Crick and James Watson, were working, sometimes secretly, at the Cavendish Laboratory in Cambridge, England.

The young men were much in awe of the wizard of Caltech but in the end they bested him. Pauling proposed a triple helix model with a particular arrangement of atoms. He was wrong. In 1953, in Crick and Watson's laboratory, he saw a model of a double helix DNA molecule and knew at once that the puzzle was solved. One of the great scientific discoveries of the twentieth century had slipped away from him, although he had helped to build toward it.

Life for Linus Pauling was no longer a simple obstacle course. It was a roller coaster, catapulting to this depth of defeat and rising to the height of triumph.

Just a year after Crick and Watson's discovery of the double helix, Pauling was called from a classroom to be told by telephone that he had been awarded the Nobel Prize in Chemistry for his work on the chemical bond. Later to the Stockholm students who paraded in honor of the Nobel laureates, he said "always be skeptical—always think for yourself." "Never put your trust in anything but your own intellect."

His campaign against war and atomic bomb testing went on. Many scientists supported him. Some still ardently opposed. One day, in 1962, with his usual boldness, he picketed the White House as a witness against testing. That evening he entered the White House as a guest at a banquet hosted by President John Kennedy to honor outstanding Americans.

On October 10, 1963, Pauling's long-cherished dream, an international treaty banning atmospheric nuclear testing, went into effect. The next day he received a call at a ranger station near his ranch on the California coast. He had been awarded the Nobel Prize for Peace. Marie Curie had shared her first Nobel. Pauling had become the first person ever to receive two un-shared Nobels and for him the second prize was of greater value than the first.

Pauling was sixty-years old, both highly honored, and fiercely criticized. Even now his life of controversy was not ended.

He left his long-time academic home at Caltech where his political activities had made many of his colleagues uneasy. After a few wandering years he co-founded his own Linus Pauling Institute of Science and Medicine in Palo Alto, California.

In his old age he took up his last ardent campaign, "orthomolecular medicine" — the use of vitamins and other natural substances to maintain human health. As a result of that campaign, he became known as "the Vitamin C Man" to the general public, unfamiliar with his many other achievements.

Although Linus Pauling was not the discoverer of Vitamin C, in the 1970's he became convinced that the vitamin could cure not only scurvy, as had been known for years, but many other diseases. He lectured widely and wrote a series of impassioned popular books entitled

Vitamins C and the Common Cold, Vitamin C, the Common Cold and Flu, and *Cancer and Vitamin C.*

Vitamin C did not save his beloved wife, Ava Helen, who died of cancer in 1981. Despite his grief, his faith in his natural wonder pill was unshaken. He went on writing and lecturing, still a striking figure, tall, slender, with intense blue eyes and a black beret poised above thinning, curly hair.

Many scientists derided his "orthomolecular" medicine. Doctors attacked him for invading a field not his own as doctors had once attacked Louis Pasteur. Like Pasteur, Pauling had never stayed within the boundaries of a single discipline and he never turned his back on battle.

The controversy over Vitamin C continues today. Many researchers scoff at Pauling's claim for its curative and preventive powers. Some consider that large quantities of the vitamin do real harm. Others present new evidence that Pauling was right. The public seems to have voted with him. Vitamin pills continue to crowd drug store shelves.

Even so restless and curious a man must bow at last to time.

Tended by his children, Pauling died in 1994 at his Big Sur ranch. He was ninety-three years old.

During his long and vigorous life he had always delighted in his work and pitied people who knew nothing about chemistry. They missed one of life's great joys— understanding and probing the world about them.

He loved the history of his science. As a good storyteller, he often spoke to his audiences about great discoveries and great chemists of the past. Historians of the future will surely speak of Linus Pauling, the man whom many consider to have been the greatest chemist of the twentieth century.

What Next?

A boy in love with science recently mourned that all the important discoveries had been made.

An experienced older researcher said, "We have answered only the easy questions."

Ahead lie alluring secrets. The mystery-solvers of the future will, like those who have gone before, be afire with energy and curiosity. They will be women and men of all races. Some will spring from people who have in the past had little access to laboratories. Many will be young— too young to believe that some things "cannot" be done.

The most startling future discoveries may lie hidden in the minds of those just beginning a life in science— or in the minds of scientists yet unborn. These discoveries are unpredictable.

It _is_ predictable that chemists of the future, among other ventures, will:

- investigate the basis of human consciousness. Why do I know myself to be a separate person? Why do I experience the world in my own way?

- invent new materials, some in space laboratories, some on earth. They may use "buckyballs," recently discovered molecules made up of sixty carbon atoms arranged in soccer ball shape. They may use tiny "nanotubes," also of carbon. "Nanotubes", only twelve atoms in diameter, may turn out to form materials ten times as strong as steel.

- explore the Island of Stability. The Old Testament mentions six materials which we now call elements. The ancient world knew nine. Lavoisier listed thirty-three, although he made some mistakes. Mendeleyev recognized sixty-three and predicted more. In 1999, nuclear chemists at the Lawrence Berkeley National Laboratory in California brought the number to 118. The heaviest elements, man-made in giant atom-smashers, have not been found occurring naturally on earth, although they may once have been here. A few have life spans of an eye-blink. Some, though not all, theoretical chemists predict a useful Island of Stability. On that Island may be elements with very long lives and properties as amazing — perhaps as terrifying — as those of plutonium, number 94. Plutonium, discovered in the debris of the first thermonuclear explosion, has been used in the atom bomb and in space craft propellants.

- complete the human genome project, mapping the location of all the genes in the human DNA molecule. Difficulties are daunting, but gene replacement therapy may one day end inherited diseases.

- seek safe, non-contaminating ways to store nuclear and industrial waste, a pressing problem not solved in the twentieth century.

- add to the existing 14,000,000 chemical compounds, natural and man-made!

Perhaps most important of all, chemists could swiftly join with other scientists, with governments, industries and citizens world-wide to prevent the environmental catastrophes which Linus Pauling and others have predicted as threats to life on earth. If chemists act wisely, they may well earn for their profession the old title of "divine", not "swindler", science.

My special thanks go to the Carnegie Library of Pittsburgh and the Hillman Library of the University of Pittsburgh. Both libraries, essential to the writing of this book, have been invaluable to me over many years.

Bibliography

Asimov, Issac. *Asimov's Biographical Encyclopedia of Science and Technology*. Avon Press, New York, 1976.

Bernhard, Carl Gustaf. *Through France with Berzelius*. Pergamon Press, Oxford and New York, 1989.

Ed. Brasted, Robert C. and Farago, Peter. "Interview with Dorothy Crowfoot Hodgkin." *Journal of Chemical Education*, v.54, no. 4, April 1977.

Brock, William H. *Justus von Liebig*. Cambridge University Press, Cambridge, Massachusetts, 1997.

Burns, Ralph A. *Essentials of Chemistry*. Second Edition. Prentice Hall, Englewood Cliffs, New Jersey, 1995.

Ed. Cardwell, D.S.L. *John Dalton and the Progress of Science*. Manchester University Press, and Barnes and Noble Inc., New York, 1968.

Clark, John Ruskin. *Joseph Priestley, A Comet in the System*. Torch Publications, San Diego, 1990. (Reprinted by Friends of Joseph Priestley House, 1994)

Cuny, Hilaire. *Louis Pasteur*. Souvenir Press, London, 1963.

Curie, Eve. *Madame Curie*. Garden City Publishing Co., Garden City, New York, 1940.

Davis, Kenneth Sydney. *The Cautionary Scientists: Priestley, Lavoisier, and the Founding of Modern Chemistry*. Putnam, New York, 1966.

Debre, Patrice. *Louis Pasteur*. Johns Hopkins University Press, Baltimore and London, 1994.

Dubos, Rene. *Pasteur and Modern Science*. Doubleday and Company, Inc., Garden City, New York, 1960.

Farber, Edward. *Great Chemists*. Interscience Publishers, New York, 1961.

French, Sydney J. *Torch and Crucible*. Princeton University Press, Princeton, New Jersey, 1941.

Gibbs, F.W. *Joseph Priestley*. Thomas Nelson and Sons, Ltd., London, 1965.

Ed. Gillespie, Charles Coulston. *Dictionary of Scientific Biography*. Charles Scribner's Sons, New York, 1970-1976.

Grady, Sean M. *The Importance of Marie Curie*. Lucent Books, San Diego, 1992.

Graham, Jenny. *Revolutionary in Exile*. American Philosophical Society, Philadelphia, 1995.

Greenaway, Frank. *John Dalton and the Atom*. Cornell University Press, Ithaca, New York, 1963.

Gueriac, Henry. *Lavoisier—The Crucial Year*. Cornell University, Ithaca, New York, 1961.

Hager, Thomas. *Force of Nature*. Simon and Schuster, New York, 1995.

Jorpes, J. Erik. *Jacob Berzelius, His Life and Work*. Almquist & Wiksell, Upsala, Sweden, 1966.

Julian, Maureen M. "Dorothy Crowfoot Hodgkin, Nobel Laureate." *Journal of Chemical Education*, v. 59, no 2, February 1982.

Ed. Magill, Frank N. *The Nobel Prize Winners in Chemistry*. Salem Press, Pasadena, 1990.

Malhado, Evan M. *Jacob Berzelius*. University of Wisconsin Press, Wisconsin, 1981.

McKie, Douglas. *Antoine Lavosier, The Father of Modern Chemistry*. J.B. Lippincott Company, Philadelphia, 1935.

Ed. McMurray, Emily J. *Notable Twentieth-Century Scientists*. Gale Research, Detroit, Michigan, 1995.

Ed. Melhado, Evan M and Frangsmyr, Tore. *Enlightenment Science in the Romantic Era*. Cambridge University Press, Cambridge, Massachusetts 1992.

Mendeleyev, D. *The Principles of Chemistry*. Longmans, Green, London and New York, 1905.

Millington, J.P. *John Dalton*. E.P. Dutton, New York, 1906.

Nicolle, Jacques. *Louis Pasteur*. Basic Books, Inc. New York, 1961.

Opfell, Olga S. *The Lady Laureates*. Scarecrow Press, Metuchen, New Jersey, 1993.

Partington, J.R. *A History of Chemistry*, Volume Four. Macmillan & Company, London, 1964.

Partington, J. R. *A Short History of Chemistry*. Harper Torchbooks, New York, 1960.

Patterson, Elizabeth C. *John Dalton and The Atomic Theory*. Doubleday & Company, Inc., Garden City, New York, 1970.

Pflaum, Rosalynd. *Grand Obsession, Madame Curie and Her World*. Doubleday, New York, 1989.

Pizarzhevskii, Oleg Nikolaevich. *Dimitrii Ivanovich Mendeleyev, His Life and Work*. Foreign Language Publishing House, 1954.

Poirier, Jean-Pierre. *Lavoisier, Chemist, Biologist, Economist*. University of Pennsylvania Press, Philadelphia, 1993.

Posin, Daniel Q. *Mendeleyev, The Story of a Great Scientist*. Whittlesey House, New York, 1948.

Priestley, Joseph. *Memoirs of Dr. Joseph Priestley*. Kraus Reprint Company, Millwood, New York, 1978.

Quinn, Susan. *Marie Curie, a Life*. Simon and Schuster, New York, 1995.

Reid, Robert W. *Marie Curie*. E.P. Dutton and Company, New York, 1974.

Roscoe, Henry E. *John Dalton and The Rise of Modern Chemistry*. MacMillan and Company, New York, 1895.

Ed. Schofield, Robert E. *A Scientific Autobiography of Joseph Priestley*. M.I.T. Press, Cambridge, Massachusetts, 1996.

Serafini, Anthony. *Linus Pauling: A Man and his Science*. Paragon House, New York, 1989.

Thackray, Arnold. *John Dalton. Harvard University Press*, Cambridge, Massachusetts, 1972.

Thorpe, T.E. *Joseph Priestley*. E.P. Dutton, New York, 1906.

Uvarov, E.B. and Isaacs, Alan. *Dictionary of Science*. Seventh Edition. Penguin Books, Ltd. London, 1993.

Vallery-Radot, Maurice. *Pasteur*. Pierre-Marcel Favre, Lausanne, Suisse, 1985.

Willstätter, Richard. *From My Life*. W.A. Benjamin, Inc. New York and Amsterdam, 1965.

Index